GW00838552

THE ASHES
PLAYER BY PLAYER

First published in the UK in 2013

© Demand Media Limited 2013

www.demand-media.co.uk

All rights reserved. No part of this work may be reproduced or utilised in any form or by any means, electronic or mechanical, including photocopying, recording or by any information storage and retrieval system, without prior written permission of the publisher.

Printed and bound in China.

ISBN 978-1-909217-25-6

The views in this book are those of the author but they are general views only and readers are urged to consult the relevant and qualified specialist for individual advice in particular situations. Demand Media Limited hereby exclude all liability to the extent permitted by law of any errors or omissions in this book and for any loss, damage or expense (whether direct or indirect) suffered by a third party relying on any information contained in this book.

All our best endeavours have been made to secure copyright clearance for every photograph used but in the event of any copyright owner being overlooked please address correspondence to Demand Media Limited, Waterside Chambers, Bridge Barn Lane, Woking, Surrey, GU21 6NL

CONTENTS

4 Introduction

ENGLAND

Page	Letter	Players
8	A	Ames, Anderson, Atherton
9	B	Bailey, Barnes, Barrington, Bedser, Botham, Boycott, Brearley
20	C	Compton, Cook, Cowdrey
24	D	Dexter
25	E	Edrich, Emburey, Evans
28	F	Flintoff
30	G	Gatting, Gooch, Gough, Gower, Greig
35	H	Hammond, Hayward, Hendren, Hobbs, Hussain, Hutton
43	K	Knott
45	L	Laker, Larwood, Lilley
49	M	MacLaren, May
51	P	Peel, Pietersen
53	R	Rhodes
54	S	Snow, Statham, Stewart, Sutcliffe
58	T	Tate, Taylor, Trueman
62	U	Underwood
63	V	Vaughan, Verity
66	W	Willis, Woolley

AUSTRALIA

Page	Letter	Players
68	A	Alderman
69	B	Benaud, Boon, Border, Bradman,
76	C	Chappell, Chappell, Clarke
79	D	Davidson
80	G	Gilchrist, Gregory, Grimmett, Grout
84	H	Harvey, Hassett, Hayden, Healy, Hill, Hogg, Hughes
91	L	Langer, Lawry, Lawson, Lillee, Lindwall
98	M	Macartney, Mailey, Marsh, Massie, McCabe, McGrath, McKenzie, Miller, Morris
107	O	O'Reily
108	P	Ponsford, Ponting
110	S	Simpson, Slater, Spofforth
113	T	Taylor, Thomson, Trumble, Trumper, Turner
118	W	Walters, Warne, Waugh, Waugh, Woodfull

24 S SERIE 010/11

Introduction

Every couple of years, the cricket authorities of Australia and England assemble their best players to vie for what might be termed the tiniest 'trophy' in world sport. Although it resides permanently in the MCC museum at Lord's, the six-inch high urn said to contain the ashes of English cricket – done to death when Australia triumphed in an 1881 Test match at The Oval – embodies the colossal and continuing struggle for supremacy between the two countries.

It was something of a joke to begin with. After that momentous Aussie victory, in the ninth match played between the two nations, a tongue-in-cheek obituary appeared in The Sporting Times 'in affectionate remembrance of English cricket'. The body would be cremated, the notice informed readers, and the ashes taken to Australia. To prolong the joke, an urn – containing the charred remains of a bail, it's said – was presented to England captain Ivo Bligh in Melbourne in 1883, and 'The Ashes' have been fought over ever since.

Nowadays, victorious captains hold aloft replicas of the real urn, but the contest itself is very real.

And what a contest this tussle for a largely symbolic prize has turned out to be. As we wait impatiently for the 2013 and 2013/14 series to unfold, England have

their hands firmly on the 'trophy', having won the last two series. But they have some way to go if they are to overtake Australia's record of 123 victories in the 310 Ashes Tests played so far. England have claimed 100 wins and the remaining 87 matches have been drawn.

THE ASHES
back with the urn, the urn;
Read and Tylecote return,
will ring loud,
crowd will feel proud,
and Bates with the urn,
coming home with the urn.

Along the way, the Ashes have thrown up some of cricket's most heroic stories, have captivated and anguished huge crowds far beyond the borders of the competing countries, and have starred some of the greatest cricketers ever to strap on a batting pad. This book celebrates those cricketers.

It is, of course, devilishly difficult to choose just fifty players from each side to represent the many hundreds who have valiantly given battle in The Ashes. The constraints of space mean that some giants of the game have had to be omitted. It must also be said that some cricketers who made their reputations in non-Ashes series failed to shine, for whatever reason, when it came to taking on the old enemy. But the stories of the players featured in this book compensate many times over for any omissions.

Cricket enthusiasts of recent decades have been privileged to witness the incredible contests of 1981 – dubbed Botham's Ashes following the all-rounder's extraordinary exploits with bat and ball – and 2005, when Andrew Flintoff threatened to eclipse even that sublime performance. Further back in Ashes history, the 1948 series shines out as one of the Australians' greatest

moments; they left English shores unbeaten, acclaimed as the Invincibles and with Don Bradman having ended his Test career with a batting average of 99.94. Then there were was the infamous Bodyline Tour of 1932/33, when England attempted to tame Bradman with dubious fast-bowling tactics.

The history of The Ashes is, naturally, a history of a team game. But it is also a history of players whose stories will be told as long as cricket is played. Here are some of those players and their stories.

Ames

Right: *Les Ames – the only wicketkeeper to score 100 first-class centuries*

Later described by many as the greatest English wicketkeeper-batsman of them all, Les Ames made his first-class debut for Kent in 1926, becoming a regular the following season. He was called up to England duty for the 1928/29 Ashes tour, but featured only in state games; his Test match debut came against South Africa in the summer of 1929. Ames had to wait until the 1932/33 'Bodyline' tour for his first match against Australia, and his first innings of note came when he scored 69 in the second innings at Adelaide. The following summer he knocked 120 off the Aussie attack as England recorded an innings victory at Lord's. Later in the same series he recorded a 72 at Old Trafford and, meanwhile, his tally of victims caught and stumped was mounting. As comfortable standing up to the wicket for fast bowlers as for spinners, he included a stumping off the Notts quick Bill Voce among his victims. Ames' batting average against the Aussies did not approach his overall Test match figure (40.56), but as late as 1938 he was scoring 83 in an Ashes match at Lord's. That match was to prove his last Ashes hurrah, the intervention of the war bringing an end to his international career. Wisden Cricketer of the Year in 1929, he remains the only wicketkeeper to score 100 first-class centuries and still holds the records for most wicketkeeper dismissals (129) and most stumpings (64) in an English county season. His first-class stumpings total (418) is also a record.

Born: Eltham, Kent, 3 December 1905
Died: Canterbury, Kent, 27 February 1990
Roles: Right-hand bat, wicketkeeper
Teams: Kent, England
Ashes debut: 2 December 1932, Sydney
Last Ashes appearance: 24 June 1938, Lord's
Ashes appearances: 17
Batting: 675 runs; average 27.00
Highest score: 120
Fielding: 33 caught, 4 stumped

Anderson

There have been two distinct phases in the career of Jimmy Anderson, aka the Burnley Express, aka the King of Swing. The first came when he tried to dismiss batsmen with every ball, putting immense strain on his body and his bowling average. The second started when he started to concentrate on line and length while retaining a master's ability to make the ball swing every which way. He had been hurried into the England one-day team facing Australia down under in 2002/03, and he faced mixed fortunes as his career progressed and injury intervened. His Test debut came in 2003 against Zimbabwe, but the Ashes came calling in Australia in 2006, when his series wicket haul – a mere five wickets to show for 93 overs of toil and 413 runs conceded – was modest. Ever since, though, Anderson has been a thorn in the Aussies' side. He claimed 12 wickets in the 2009 series in England, but the 2010/11 Ashes tour was a triumph: picking up wickets steadily, he finished with 24 Australian scalps, at an average of 26.04, despite never breaking the five-for barrier. In fact, he has taken five in an innings just once against the Aussies – at Edgbaston in 2009 – but his adversaries must fear there are more to come. The kind of fielder every captain wishes for, Anderson's batting has also come on in leaps and bounds since his early days, with a tense 69-minute innings at Cardiff in 2009 testifying to his stickability.

Above: *James Anderson – a constant thorn in the Australians' side*

Born: Burnley, Lancashire, 30 July 1982
Roles: Left-hand bat, right-arm fast-medium bowler
Teams: Lancashire, Auckland, England
Ashes debut: 23 November 2006, Brisbane
Last Ashes appearance: 3 January 2011, Sydney
Ashes appearances: 13
Bowling: 41 wickets; average 38.53
Best bowling: 5/80
Batting: 133 runs; average 10.23
Highest score: 29
Fielding: 6 caught

Atherton

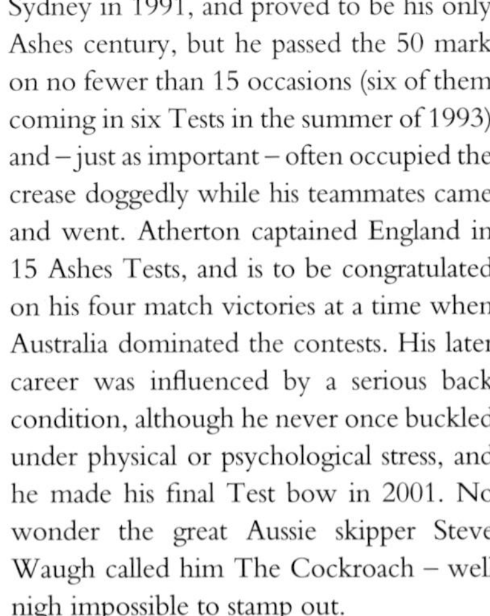

Below: *Mike Atherton – immune to opponents' sledging tactics*

All too often as the 12 years of Mike Atherton's Ashes career unfolded and the minutes he spent at the crease increased, Australian fielders stood and fumed. Here was a batsman who was immune to the taunts and subtle hints the most gifted sledger could dream up, and who treated Aussie bowlers with a gutsy stubbornness they were forced, grudgingly, to admire. Having made his name as a gifted opening bat and thoughtful skipper at Cambridge University, Atherton was earmarked early on as a future England captain, and his performances for Lancashire confirmed his potential. His first Ashes innings at Trent Bridge ended almost as early as it began, but he followed up that duck with a second-innings 47, setting down a marker in the process. His top score against the Australians came at Sydney in 1991, and proved to be his only Ashes century, but he passed the 50 mark on no fewer than 15 occasions (six of them coming in six Tests in the summer of 1993) and – just as important – often occupied the crease doggedly while his teammates came and went. Atherton captained England in 15 Ashes Tests, and is to be congratulated on his four match victories at a time when Australia dominated the contests. His later career was influenced by a serious back condition, although he never once buckled under physical or psychological stress, and he made his final Test bow in 2001. No wonder the great Aussie skipper Steve Waugh called him The Cockroach – well nigh impossible to stamp out.

Born: Failsworth, Manchester, 23 March 1968
Roles: Right-hand bat, leg break bowler
Teams: Cambridge University, Lancashire, England
Ashes debut: 10 August 1989, Nottingham
Last Ashes appearance: 23 August 2001, The Oval
Ashes appearances: 33
Batting: 1900 runs; average 29.68
Highest score: 105
Fielding: 22 caught

Bailey

The world's best all-rounder for much of his career, Trevor Bailey allied a deadly mastery of swing bowling to a stubborn reluctance to surrender his wicket and brilliant close-catching technique. He had already played for Essex when he went up to Cambridge in 1947, and he went on to earn Blues for both cricket and football. His first Test cap came in 1949, and he first locked horns with Australia, in what was to become a titanic struggle, a year later. Bailey's obdurate batting style was ideal in a crisis, and he is perhaps best remembered for a remarkable final-day partnership with Willie Watson at Lord's in 1953, when the pair resisted the Aussie attack for more than four hours to earn a draw. Later that summer, at Headingley, it was Bailey's niggardly bowling that frustrated his opponents' drive for victory and set up a tense final Test at The Oval. England won that match and with it the Ashes – for the first time in 19 years. Often opening the batting for England, he notched five half-centuries against Australia, and took four wickets in an innings four times. On his final Ashes tour, in 1958/59, he ground out the slowest ever 50 in first-class cricket, taking almost six hours to reach the mark in the first Test at Brisbane. That tour was Bailey's last for England, but he remained an important figure in the game as a player, administrator, journalist and broadcaster.

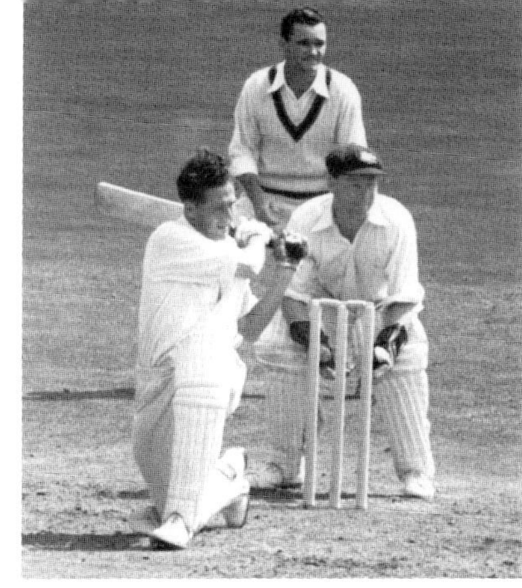

Left: *Trevor Bailey – the ideal man for a batting crisis*

Born: Westcliff-on-Sea, Essex, 3 December 1923
Died: Westcliff-on-Sea, Essex, 10 February 2011
Roles: Right-hand bat, right-arm fast-medium bowler
Teams: Cambridge University, Essex, England
Ashes debut: 1 December 1950, Brisbane
Last Ashes appearance: 13 February 1959, Melbourne
Ashes appearances: 23
Batting: 875 runs; average 25.73
Highest score: 88
Bowling: 42 wickets; average 32.69
Best bowling: 4/22
Fielding: 16 caught

Barnes

Sydney Barnes was a remarkable bowler who mixed an ability to swing the ball both ways with a disconcerting tendency to spin it to both off and leg. To add to the batsman's problems, he was adept at disguising his pace, made clever use of his height, producing prodigious lift off the pitch, and had a deadly yorker. Opponents just never knew what was coming next, and even if they could spot his intentions they were all too often helpless to counter them. Barnes spent much of his career playing league rather than county cricket, and it was from the Lancashire League that he was plucked to tour Australia in 1901/02. He took six wickets in his first Ashes test and followed up with 13 in the next, making an immediate impression on the Australians that was to lead to them dubbing him the best bowler they had ever faced. He continued to torment the Aussies until 1912, when he signed off from Ashes cricket with a return of 5 for 30 from 27 overs in the final Test at The Oval. Throughout his career, he displayed a flinty, aggressive character and a determination to find a batsman's weakness – and always to make him play the ball. Writing to commemorate Barnes' 90th birthday, John Arlott noted that cricketers who had played with or against him were in no doubt that he was the greatest bowler of all time.

Born: Smethwick, Staffordshire, 19 April 1873
Died: Chadsmoor, Staffordshire, 26 December 1967
Roles: Right-hand bat, right-arm medium and fast-medium bowler
Teams: Warwickshire, Lancashire, Staffordshire, England, Wales
Ashes debut: 13 December 1901, Sydney
Last Ashes appearance: 19 August 1912, The Oval
Ashes appearances: 20
Bowling: 106 wickets; average 21.58
Best bowling: 7/60
Batting: 210 runs; average 8.40
Highest score: 38*
Fielding: 7 caught

Left: *Sydney Barnes – always determined to find a batsman's weakness*

Barrington

Right: *Ken Barrington – compiler of the third highest score by an Englishman against Australia*

Ken Barrington reserved his best batting performances for Test match cricket, and he was especially punishing when he had Australian bowlers in his sights: his county cricket batting average of 39.87 was exceeded by his Test figure of 58.67, which was in turn surpassed by his Ashes average of 63.96. He had already been playing for Surrey for 11 years, and for England for six, when he first faced an Australian attack, but he made up for lost time by scoring 69 runs in the first Test of the summer of 1961 and ending the series with a total of 364, at an average of 45.50. Better was to follow. During England's tour down under in 1962/63, Barrington posted scores of 78, 23, 35, 0 not out, 35, 21, 63, 132 not out, 101 and 94, to give him a series total of 582 and an average of 72.75, and the Australians a headache. His highest Test score came at Manchester in 1964, when he answered Bobby Simpson's epic 311 with 256 runs of his own – the third highest score by an England batsman against Australia. And so it continued, with the dogged Barrington regularly foiling his opponents' plans, until 1968, when he suffered a heart attack while playing in a double-wicket tournament down under. Following his retirement, the jovial Barrington was a popular assistant manager on England tours, and it was on one such visit to the West Indies in 1981 that he suffered a further, fatal heart attack.

Born: Reading, Berkshire, 24 November 1930
Died: Bridgetown, Barbados, 14 March 1981
Roles: Right-hand bat, leg break bowler
Teams: Surrey, England
Ashes debut: 8 June 1961, Birmingham
Last Ashes appearance: 25 July 1968, Leeds
Ashes appearances: 23
Batting: 2111 runs; average 63.96
Highest score: 256
Bowling: 4 wickets; average 57.75
Best bowling: 2/47
Fielding: 19 caught

Bedser

Having made his first-class debut in 1939, Alec Bedser (like his twin brother Eric) had to wait for the cessation of hostilities before resuming his career. While Eric went on to enjoy a lengthy career with Surrey, Alec was the one who would write himself into Test match history and make a big impression in international and Ashes cricket. His first tour of the Antipodes came as a result of a home series against India in which his pace bowling twice took him to 11 wickets in a match. In the 1946/47 Ashes series, finding his stock inswinger to be to the liking of Aussie batsmen, he developed his 'special ball', an inswinging leg break that bamboozled even the great Don Bradman. During the 1950/51 tour down under, Bedser achieved a dominance over Australian batting that brought him 30 wickets in the series, at an average of 16.06, and he was instrumental in England regaining the Ashes in 1953 at the advanced age of 35. His total of 39 wickets in that series – which included a match haul of 14 for 99 at Trent Bridge – cost a miserly 17.48 runs each. He had spearheaded, and often carried, England's post-war bowling attack, in the process becoming the leading Test wicket-taker with a total of 236. His influence on the game continued after his retirement as he became a Test match selector and then chairman of selectors from 1969 to 1981.

Above: *Alec Bedser – capable of bamboozling the greatest of all batsmen*

Born: Reading, Berkshire, 4 July 1918
Died: Woking, Surrey, 4 April 2010
Roles: Right-hand bat, right-arm medium-fast bowler
Teams: Surrey, England
Ashes debut: 13 December 1946, Sydney
Last Ashes appearance: 15 August 1953, The Oval
Ashes appearances: 21
Bowling: 104 wickets; average 27.49
Best bowling: 7/44
Batting: 373 runs; average 14.34
Highest score: 79
Fielding: 11 caught

Botham

Right: *Ian Botham – fiercely competitive, and relished the challenge of matches against Australia*

Ian Botham's first and last Test appearances against Australia came 12 years apart at Trent Bridge. In between, he bestrode the Ashes stage like a latter-day Colossus, at times achieving almost mythical status. A genuine all-rounder who could shred any attack with the bat one day and whistle through a batting order with the ball the next, he was a strong-minded performer who relished the challenge of battles against the steely Aussies. He had a solid, classical batting technique, which he allied to tremendous hitting power, and his swing bowling was similarly based on sound principles. Botham's first few Ashes matches revealed his bowling talent but his first century did not arrive until 1980 in Melbourne. Then, the following year, in the series known ever after as Botham's Ashes, he set the summer alight with incredible, match-winning performances with bat and ball. Extraordinarily ferocious innings of 149 not out and 118 at Headingley and Old Trafford were complemented by

Born: Heswall, Cheshire, 24 November 1955
Roles: Right-hand bat, right-arm fast-medium bowler
Teams: Somerset, Queensland, Worcestershire, Durham, England
Ashes debut: 28 July 1977, Nottingham
Last Ashes appearance: 10 August 1989, Nottingham
Ashes appearances: 36
Batting: 1673 runs; average 29.35
Highest score: 149*
Bowling: 148 wickets; average 27.65
Best bowling: 6/78
Fielding: 57 caught

Left: *Botham was capable of destroying any bowling attack*

vicious, Aussie-wrecking spells with the ball, and he finished the series – which England won 3-1 – with 34 wickets and 399 runs. The Botham legend had been established, although, naturally enough, he could never reach such heights again. A brilliant slip fielder, he ended his England career with 120 catches to go with his 383 wickets and 5200 runs. Against Australia, he hit four centuries, took 57 catches and claimed five wickets or more in an innings nine times. It should be no surprise that he is regarded as England cricket's finest all-rounder.

Boycott

Below: *Geoff Boycott – obsessive concentration allowed him to bat for long stretches*

Like that other cricket-playing 'B' Ian Botham, Geoff Boycott was part of the Mike Brearley-led England side that broke Australian hearts with that 3-1 Ashes victory in 1981. There the similarity with 'Beefy' ends. Where Botham smote the ball to all corners of the ground, Boycott was capable of sticking around for hours or days at a stretch, accumulating runs with rigorously correct technique, a pleasing back-foot shot through the covers and a patience bordering on obsession. In the Ashes Test at Perth in 1978, he scored 77 runs without once hitting a boundary. An opening bat of impeccable technique, dedicated to constant practice, he was content to let the runs come – and come they did. Having scored 48 in his first innings against the Australians and registered his first Ashes century at The Oval in 1964, Boycott set about his run-gathering with unwavering concentration. The fact that he seemed sometimes to be playing for Geoff Boycott rather than England, and was involved in more than one controversial run-out, made him less popular than he might have been, but when he scored his hundredth first-class century for England against the Australians, at his home ground of Headingley, the nation rose to applaud. He finished his career with seven centuries against the Aussies, out of a Test match total of 22, and a look back at the statistics confirms the importance of Boycott to his country: in his 108 Tests he was on the losing side a mere 20 times.

Born: Fitzwilliam, Yorkshire, 21 October 1940
Roles: Right-hand bat, right-arm medium bowler
Teams: Yorkshire, Northern Transvaal, England
Ashes debut: 4 June 1964, Nottingham
Last Ashes appearance: 27 August 1981, The Oval
Ashes appearances: 38
Batting: 2945 runs; average 47.50
Highest score: 191
Bowling: 2 wickets; average 53.50
Best bowling: 2/32
Fielding: 12 caught

Brearley

If the only criteria for entry in this book were excellence with bat, ball or both, Mike Brearley would not have stood the slightest chance of inclusion. It would be generous to describe his Test match batting record as mediocre, and his performances in Ashes matches did nothing to improve it. His ability to snaffle catches in the slips was outstanding, but where he really excelled was in captaincy, in which his inspired man management and mastery of the arts of psychology sometimes worked miracles. Brearley had had a more than respectable career with Cambridge University and Middlesex before he first took charge of the national team in 1977 having earned his first cap the previous year, when he was 34. He then passed on the captaincy to Ian Botham in 1980. Taking over once again from a demoralised Botham following the latter's resignation after the second Ashes Test in 1981, he called upon all his motivational knowhow to raise the great all-rounder from the doldrums and inspire fast bowler Bob Willis to previously unimagined feats. From appearing doomed to defeat at the third Test at Headingley, England rose as one man and simply swatted Australia out of the way, with Botham and Willis leading the fightback. Meanwhile, the thoughtful, unassuming Brearley could be seen on the edge of the picture, exhorting, applauding, cajoling, urging his players on to ever greater effort. England went on to win the series 3-1, whereupon Brearley again stepped back into the shadows, his reputation as one of the game's best skippers assured.

Above: *Mike Brearley – his man management gifts sometimes wrought miracles*

Born: Harrow, Middlesex, 28 April 1942
Roles: Right-hand bat
Teams: Cambridge University, Middlesex, England
Ashes debut: 12 March 1977, Melbourne
Last Ashes appearance: 27 August 1981, The Oval
Ashes appearances: 19
Batting: 798 runs; average 22.80
Highest score: 81
Fielding: 20 caught

Compton

Below: *Denis Compton – amazing summer of 1947 is still the talk of cricket fans*

No sportsman helped the British discover their post-war optimism quite like Denis Compton; few have ever exhibited such joie de vivre in pursuing their calling. A talented footballer who played more than 50 times for Arsenal, he also found time to earn 78 England caps at cricket and nail down a reputation as one of the country's greatest batsmen, capable of thrilling crowds with dazzling strokeplay all round the wicket. Some of his best performances came in Ashes matches, starting with his debut innings at the age of 19, when he scored 102 against Don Bradman's tourists. After the war Compton continued to pile up runs in wonderful fashion, and his annus mirabilis of 1947, when he totalled 3816 runs, is still discussed in awed tones. In the preceding tour of Australia he had registered centuries in each innings of the Adelaide Test, and in the 1948 series in England he scored 562 runs at an average of 62.44, against one of the fiercest bowling attacks ever mustered. That total included an innings of 184 at Trent Bridge that threatened to avert an inevitable Australian victory and a further century at Old Trafford after he had been hit on the head by a Ray Lindwall bouncer. Hampered by a knee injury, he never attained those heights again, but he finished with five Ashes hundreds, the adulation of a nation's cricket fans and a grandson, Nick, who would go on to play for England.

Born: Hendon, Middlesex, 23 May 1918
Died: Windsor, Berkshire, 23 April 1997
Roles: Right-hand bat, left-arm slow chinamen
Teams: Middlesex, Holkar, England
Ashes debut: 10 June 1938, Nottingham
Last Ashes appearance: 23 August 1956, The Oval
Ashes appearances: 28
Batting: 1842 runs; average 42.83
Highest score: 184
Bowling: 3 wickets, average 99.33
Best bowling: 1/18
Fielding: 17 caught

Cook

Followers of Alastair Cook, England Test captain and opening bat, have every reason to look forward to the summer/winter Ashes showdowns of 2013 and 2013/2014. The prodigiously gifted young left-hander has already achieved more than most players do in a lifetime, and shows every sign of continuing to break records. In the six short years since his Test debut, Cook has amassed 7,117 runs at an average of 49.42, and compiled 23 centuries (a record for an England player) and 29 fifties. And his record against Australia is, if anything, even better: in his 26 Ashes innings he has passed 100 four times and 50 on three further occasions, leaving him with an average over 50. But these bald figures mask the reality of what promises to be the most extraordinary Test career of any Englishman, ever. By the time he was 25, Cook had scored many more runs and centuries than any other compatriot; he was the youngest player of any nationality to pass 7000 Test runs; and he was the first cricketer to score a century in each of his first five Tests as captain.

Above: *Alastair Cook – a record breaker, and still so much to give*

Born: Gloucester, 25 December 1984
Roles: Left-hand bat, right-arm off spin
Teams: Essex, England
Ashes debut: 23 November 2006, Brisbane
Ashes appearances: 15
Batting: 1264 runs; average 50.56
Highest score: 235*
Fielding: 14 caught

Above: *Alastair Cook (right) and captain Andrew Strauss celebrate with the urn after winning the 2010/11 Ashes series*

The Australians have only to think back to the Ashes series of 2010/2011 to realise what a threat Cook represents. He batted a mere seven times in those five matches, yet scored the amazing total of 766 runs, including three centuries and two fifties, while occupying the crease for 2171 minutes, a world record for a five-match series. The Aussies can hardly be consoled by the thought that he is perhaps yet to reach his prime. Cook still has so much to give.

Cowdrey

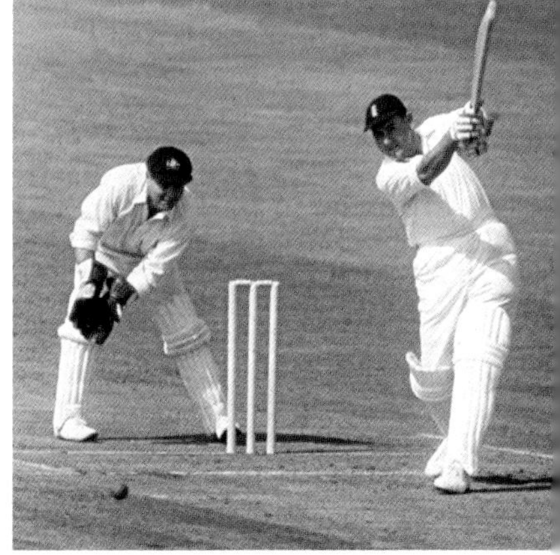

Above: *Colin Cowdrey – stylish performer with the bat and terrific slip catcher*

When Colin Cowdrey's parents gave him the initials MCC, the same as those of the world's pre-eminent club, they might have been giving warning that a mighty cricket talent had been born. The young Cowdrey – later Sir Colin and later still Lord Cowdrey – fulfilled every bit of promise his naming and early performances had shown, and long before he retired after a 26-year career he had been acclaimed as one of England's foremost batsmen. The figures and records speak for themselves: Cowdrey scored 7624 Test match runs at an average of 44.06, with a top score of 182; he went past the 100 mark 22 times, a joint record before Alastair Cook beat it recently. He toured Australia six times, the first time as a 21-year-old, the last at the age of 41. First time out his 319 runs in the series included a first-innings 109 at Melbourne, and four further hundreds were to follow in Ashes Tests. A late call-up to his last series down under saw him, with a mere two days' practice under his belt, facing Dennis Lillee and Jeff Thomson at their fastest and most aggressive on a poor pitch at Perth. His flawless technique and cool courage saw him score 22 and 41 and earn the undying respect of all who were there. Cowdrey, who captained England 27 times, was a consummate stylist with a delicious cover drive and perfect timing who served his country with distinction, and every honour he received was richly deserved.

Born: Bangalore, India, 24 December 1932
Died: Angmering Park, Sussex, 4 December 2000
Roles: Right-hand bat, right-arm leg spin bowler
Teams: Oxford University, Kent, England
Ashes debut: 26 November 1954, Brisbane
Last Ashes appearance: 13 February 1975, Melbourne
Ashes appearances: 43
Batting: 2433 runs; average 34.26
Highest score: 113
Fielding: 40 caught

Dexter

Below: *Ted Dexter – aggression and power allied to self-assurance and solid technique*

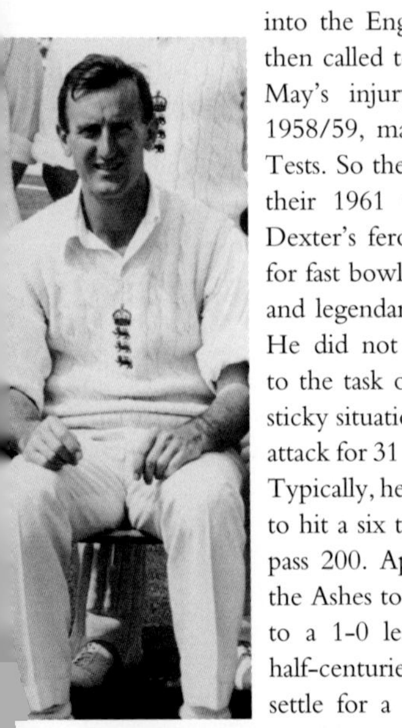

Having played his way through private school and Cambridge University swinging his bat in much the same way as he wielded a driver on the golf course (another favourite occupation at which he excelled), Ted Dexter eased into the England team in 1958. He was then called to Australia to reinforce Peter May's injury-stricken touring team of 1958/59, making no great impression in Tests. So the Australians had to wait until their 1961 tour of England to witness Dexter's ferocious hitting power, disdain for fast bowling – any bowling, actually – and legendary self-assurance at first hand. He did not disappoint, applying himself to the task of extricating his team from a sticky situation by thrashing the Australian attack for 31 boundaries on his way to 180. Typically, he fell to a stumping while trying to hit a six to put himself in a position to pass 200. Appointed England captain for the Ashes tour of 1962/63, he led his side to a 1-0 lead, scoring four consecutive half-centuries along the way, but had to settle for a drawn series. Dexter, always showing his natural aggression and raw power, scored a second Ashes century at Old Trafford in 1964 and, when he retired in 1968, closed his account with Australia with eight other scores of fifty-plus to his credit. His detractors point to his relative lack of success as a captain. Enthusiasts point to his aptitude for one-day cricket and wonder what destruction 'Lord Ted' might have wrought in today's game.

Born: Milan, Italy, 15 May 1935
Roles: Right-hand bat, right-arm medium bowler
Teams: Cambridge University, Sussex, England
Ashes debut: 8 June 1961, Birmingham
Last Ashes appearance: 27 August 1968, The Oval
Ashes appearances: 19
Batting: 1358 runs; average 38.80
Highest score: 180
Bowling: 23 wickets, average 32.26
Best bowling: 3/16
Fielding: 10 caught

Edrich

Left: *John Edrich – great courage and stubborn determination*

The youngest scion of a notable cricket family – his best-known relative was cousin Bill – John Edrich had a simple approach to his role as an opening bat: stay in line, don't give your wicket away and wait for the right ball to put away. Allied to stubborn determination and great courage, it was a philosophy that served him outstandingly well over a 13-year England career; never more so than at Headingley in 1965, when he punished the New Zealand attack for eight hours in scoring 310 not out. Even the great Australian fast bowler Dennis Lillee at his best couldn't knock him out of his stride or break his composure. During the first Test of the 1974/75 Ashes tour, a Lillee delivery broke bones in one of Edrich's hands. In the fourth Test, Lillee turned his attention to his adversary's ribs, breaking two of them. In both cases, Edrich returned after treatment to continue his innings. Ten years previously, on his Ashes debut at Lord's, the Surrey opener had scored 120, and he had followed up with innings of 109, 103 and 85 during the 1965/66 tour down under. He continued to score heavily against the Australians throughout his career, even hitting 82 match-winning runs when the scheduled third Test in 1970/71 was reduced to a 40-over-a-side contest. In all, Edrich recorded seven Ashes centuries out of a total of 12 in Test cricket, and came agonisingly close in his final match against Australia, scoring 96 in helping to save England from an innings defeat. It was a typical battling performance.

Born: Blofield, Norfolk, 21 June 1937
Roles: Left-hand bat, right-arm medium bowler
Teams: Surrey, England
Ashes debut: 18 June 1964, Lord's
Last Ashes appearance: 3 September 1975, The Oval
Ashes appearances: 32
Batting: 2644 runs; average 48.96
Highest score: 175
Fielding: 16 caught

Emburey

Below: *John Emburey (left) with Mike Gatting – steady probing brought him 78 Ashes wickets*

It was perhaps John Emburey's misfortune that he flourished at a time when spin bowling was not as highly valued an occupation as it was before he emerged, and is now. Still, with his steady probing with his off breaks, his awkward bounce and the occasional arm ball, he carved himself a niche in the England side that brought him 147 Test match wickets and made an impression on Ashes cricket that the Australians are unlikely to forget for a long time. He claimed 16 victims in his first Ashes series, in 1978/79, and followed up with 18 in his second, in 1986/87. The latter haul included his best return of 7 for 78, from 46 overs with 15 maidens, at the Sydney Test, when he was bowling, as he often did back home at Lord's, in tandem with his Middlesex spin partner Phil Edmonds. Emburey, a tall, thoughtful man with a classical, high bowling action, was a more than capable fielder who also found batting against Australia especially to his liking. Despite his eccentric technique, which owed more to intuition and improvisation than the coaching manual, his lower-order accumulation of runs led to the unwanted distinction of being England's highest run scorer without a Test match century to his name. He would have scored more Test runs, and taken more wickets, if he had not chosen to miss two winters by going to South Africa in 1981/82 and 1989/90 with the 'rebel' tourists.

Born: Peckham, London, 20 August 1952
Roles: Right-hand bat, right-arm off spin bowler
Teams: Middlesex, Northamptonshire, Western Province, England
Ashes debut: 29 December 1978, Melbourne
Last Ashes appearance: 9 August 1993, Birmingham
Ashes appearances: 25
Bowling: 78 wickets; average 34.58
Best bowling: 7/78
Batting: 759 runs; average 28.11
Highest score: 69
Fielding: 15 caught

Evans

Godfrey Evans could have been a contender as a boxer. His razor-sharp reflexes served him well in the ring, just as they did later in the Test match arena, as many a stumping victim could testify. His lightning reactions also amazed Australian batsman Neil Harvey at Melbourne in 1950. Standing up to Alec Bedser's fast-medium bowling, Evans had a split second to fling himself to his left and snap up Harvey's leg glance one-handed, horizontal in the air. It was that kind of wicketkeeping – often spectacular, always safe – that convinced observers that he was the best there ever was. In a 91-match Test match career that lost six years to the second world war – he had made his Kent debut in 1939 – he caught 173 victims and stumped 46, and weighed in with nearly 2500 runs, including two centuries. A measure of his quality is the fact that Australia had scored more than 1000 runs in Evans' first two Ashes Tests in the 1946/47 series before he conceded a bye. He continued in a similar vein throughout his Ashes career, meanwhile contributing to the England batting cause with sometimes thrilling, sometimes stubborn knocks. An example of the former type came in England's only innings at Old Trafford in 1956 – the match in which Jim Laker took his never-equalled 19 for 90 – when Evans rattled off 47 runs in a mere 29 minutes, with two sixes and five fours among his total. But it is as a wicketkeeper of unparalleled ability that he will always be remembered.

Born: Finchley, London, 18 August 1920
Died: Northampton, 3 May 1999
Roles: Right-hand bat, wicketkeeper
Teams: Kent, England
Ashes debut: 13 December 1946, Sydney
Last Ashes appearance: 30 January 1959, Adelaide
Ashes appearances: 31
Batting: 783 runs; average 17.79
Highest score: 50
Fielding: 64 caught, 12 stumped

Above: *Godfrey Evans – sometimes spectacular, always safe*

Flintoff

Right: *Andrew Flintoff – never one to do things by halves*

Far Right: *Let the celebrations commence – Andrew Flintoff enjoyed every minute of the post-Ashes festivities in 2005*

If you're looking for an Ashes career of light and shade, look no further than the highs and lows of Andrew Flintoff, all-rounder extraordinaire. One minute named Man of the Series for his fairy-tale exploits in the fabulous series of 2005, in which he came close to rivalling the derring-do of 1981-vintage Ian Botham; the next skippering England to a crushing 0-5 loss in Australia in 2006/07 in which he could do precious little with either bat or ball; then rising from those Ashes to help inflict another defeat on the Aussies in 2009 and bring the urn back to England. Flintoff was never one to do things by halves. Thanks to injury he was seven years into his Test career when he first faced Australia in that thrilling summer of 2005, but he made up for lost time with 24 wickets, 402 runs, some simply superb displays of destructive batting and fearsome bowling and the grateful thanks of the English people. Wrongly selected to captain the Ashes tour of 2006/07, he watched as the dream fell apart. But Flintoff, who seemed always to be on the verge of career-ending injury,

surged back in 2009. His brilliant run-out of Australian captain Ricky Ponting at The Oval did as much as anything to return the Ashes to English keeping, although his contributions with bat and ball were scarcely negligible. And that was that. Flintoff retired from Test cricket with his reputation as one of England's most exciting cricketers intact.

Born: Preston, Lancashire, 6 December 1977
Roles: Right-hand bat, right-arm fast bowler
Teams: Lancashire, England
Ashes debut: 21 July 2005, Lord's
Last Ashes appearance: 20 August 2009, The Oval
Ashes appearances: 15
Batting: 906 runs; average 33.55
Highest score: 102
Bowling: 50 wickets; average 33.20
Best bowling: 5/78
Fielding: 4 caught

591
ASHES 2005

Gatting

Right: *Mike Gatting – on his way to another pugnacious century*

Mike Gatting will always be remembered as the victim of the stunning 'Ball of the Century', the first delivery Shane Warne ever sent down in an Ashes match. But there was an awful lot more to a career that saw Gatting captaining England to a series win in Australia, score four Ashes centuries and earn the Aussies' respect as a talented and dogged competitor. His early Test career was remarkable for the number of times he passed 50 without going on to complete a century; he had to wait until his 54th innings for a hundred to arrive. Once he got his eye in, however, his pugnacious batting took him to nine further Test hundreds and a reputation as a destroyer of spin bowling. His first ton against Australia came in the fourth Test of 1985 and helped to secure him the number four spot in the order. The following year he was in Australia captaining England, who were described by a local journalist as having only three faults – 'can't bat, can't bowl, can't field' – as they approached the first Test. Gatting led his apparently untalented men to a 2-1 series win, scoring nearly 400 runs along the way. His captaincy career was wrecked after he rowed furiously with Pakistani umpire Shakoor Rana in 1987, but he wasn't finished with Test cricket as a player. His last Ashes century came at Adelaide in 1995, batting at number three and scoring 117 as Mike Atherton led his injury-hit side to England's first Test win in Australia for eight years.

Born: Kingsbury, London, 6 June 1957
Roles: Right-hand bat, right-arm medium bowler
Teams: Middlesex, England
Ashes debut: 28 August 1980, Lord's
Last Ashes appearance: 3 February 1995, Perth
Ashes appearances: 27
Batting: 1661 runs; average 37.75
Highest score: 160
Fielding: 19 caught

Gooch

Above: *Graham Gooch – dedication to his craft made him England's leading run scorer in Tests*

Graham Gooch's Ashes debut – his Test match debut, indeed – could not have gone any worse. It came against Ian Chappell's 1975 Australians at Edgbaston, where the 21-year-old Essex batsman got a pair, caught behind each time as England were thrashed by an innings. Neither did it get much better next time out: Gooch scored six and 31 at Lord's, and was promptly dropped. His Test record was to improve immeasurably over the course of the next 20 years, however: a total of 8900 runs in 118 matches at an average of 42.58, one of the highlights his magnificent total of 456 in one match against India in 1990. England captain in 34 Tests, he will remain his country's leading run scorer until Alastair Cook and/or Kevin Pietersen overtake him. He took a long time to get going against Australia, but it was worth the wait: he eventually chalked up four Ashes centuries as well as 16 other scores over 50. His last-day 117 in the fourth Test at Adelaide in 1991 – which complemented a first-innings 87 – looked at one point as if it might take England to a highly unlikely victory target of 472. Gooch was something of a batting tearaway in his youth but learned to temper his aggression with healthy pragmatism when necessary, his upright stance, with heavy bat raised high, testifying to his dedication to perfecting his craft. Now, as England's batting coach, he is passing on his secrets to younger practitioners like his Essex compatriot Cook.

Born: Leytonstone, London, 23 July 1953
Roles: Right-hand bat, right-arm medium bowler
Teams: Essex, Western Province, England
Ashes debut: 10 July 1975, Birmingham
Last Ashes appearance: 3 February 1995, Perth
Ashes appearances: 42
Batting: 2632 runs; average 33.31
Highest score: 196
Bowling: 8 wickets; average 59.75
Best bowling: 2/16
Fielding: 29 caught

Gough

Below: *Darren Gough – took six wickets on his Ashes debut*

If ever a cricketer was likely to gain the admiration of his Australian adversaries, Darren Gough was that man. A big personality and gritty performer who could never say die, he was also a highly gifted quick bowler who made the most of a sturdy physique to develop weapons like a vicious inswinging yorker. He had been discomforting batsmen for Yorkshire for five years before he made his England debut in 1994, and he went on to become his country's leading strike bowler for much of the 1990s and into the new millennium, claiming 229 Test wickets in the process. Gough relished playing in the Ashes, and he started well (despite his team's loss to the Aussies), mopping up six wickets on his debut on the 1994/95 tour down under. That tour was to produce his best bowling performance against Australia, a six-for-49 innings return that included the important wickets of Mark Taylor, David Boon and Steve Waugh, all taken without the help of a fielder. In all, he took five or more wickets in an Ashes innings four times, out of a total of nine times in all Tests. Gough was also a handy batsman who scored 65 on his Test debut but never developed into the all-rounder supporters hoped he might be. Plagued by injury towards the end of his career, he nevertheless claimed 17 victims in his final Ashes series. He retired from all cricket in 2008 having earned the respect of all he had played against.

Born: Barnsley, South Yorkshire, 18 September 1980
Roles: Right-hand bat, right-arm fast bowler
Teams: Yorkshire, Essex, England
Ashes debut: 25 November 1994, Brisbane
Last Ashes appearance: 23 August 2001, The Oval
Ashes appearances: 17
Bowling: 74 wickets; average 30.81
Best bowling: 6/49
Batting: 240 runs; average 10.00
Highest score: 51
Fielding: 5 caught

Gower

Left: *David Gower – seeming nonchalance sometimes masked enormous talent*

The first ball David Gower faced in Test cricket, bowled by Pakistan's Liaquat Ali at Edgbaston in 1978, went the way of hundreds of others that were to follow over the next 15 years: pulled with apparent nonchalance to the boundary. Gower, a supremely elegant left-hander (and a brilliant fielder in his youth), had arrived, and by the time he had finished he had scored 8231 Test match runs in 117 matches, at an average of 44.25. Statistically, his batting against Australia was marginally better. His first Ashes century came in his third innings and was followed by eight others. The highlight of that little lot was the 215 he beat out of the Australian attack at Edgbaston in 1985 as England piled up the 595 that enabled them to win by an innings. He ended that series with 732 runs (average 81.33) under his belt, a remarkable tally that took him close to England's record-holders against Australia, Wally Hammond and Herbert Sutcliffe. Gower captained England in that Ashes-regaining series, as he did in 32 Tests in total. It was to prove the highlight of his captaincy of the national team, for England won only five of those 32, losing 18. However, despite his tendency to guide catches into slip fielders' hands from balls aimed outside off stump, and in spite of his sometimes lackadaisical approach to the game, he was one of cricket's most admired performers. No one can say what he might have achieved if he had shown the same dedication as his contemporary Graham Gooch.

Born: Tunbridge Wells, Kent, 1 April 1957
Roles: Left-hand bat, right-arm off spin
Teams: Leicestershire, Hampshire, England
Ashes debut: 1 December 1978, Brisbane
Last Ashes appearance: 1 February 1991, Perth
Ashes appearances: 42
Batting: 3269 runs; average 44.78
Highest score: 215
Fielding: 26 caught

Greig

Below: *Tony Greig – complete all-rounder and a respected commentator*

The double-Ashes year of 2013 was lent extra poignancy when 66-year-old Tony Greig, England captain turned TV commentator, succumbed to a heart attack shortly before the turn of the year.

Greig made an indelible mark on cricket as player, captain, innovator and media man, and he is mourned far beyond the countries with which he is most associated: South Africa, England and Australia. Born in South Africa to a Scottish father, he made his name with Sussex as a competitive all-rounder, mixing up his medium pace bowling with canny off spin and using his tall frame to lean into beautifully timed drives. He marked his Test and Ashes debut by scoring 119 and taking five wickets, and continued in like fashion. Greig captained England in 14 Tests (winning three and drawing six) and faced Australia as skipper on four occasions, his only defeat coming in the Centenary Test at Melbourne in 1977. He was reviled in some quarters for his covert recruitment of players for Kerry Packer's World Series Cricket, a 'crime' that riled the establishment and cost him the England captaincy. The Ashes series he played under Mike Brearley in 1977 (won 3-0 by England) was his last cricket action, and he thereafter forged a popular career as a commentator. It is as a cricketer that he is best remembered, however. He was a fighter to the last, which is precisely how he reached 3599 runs and 141 wickets in his 58 Test matches.

Born: Queenstown, South Africa, 6 October 1946
Died: Sydney, 29 December 2012
Roles: Right-hand bat, right-arm medium and off spin bowler
Teams: Border, Sussex, Eastern Province, England
Ashes debut: 8 June 1972, Manchester
Last Ashes appearance: 25 August 1977, The Oval
Ashes appearances: 21
Batting: 1303 runs; average 36.19
Highest score: 110
Bowling: 44 wickets; average 37.79
Best bowling: 4/53
Fielding: 37 caught

Hammond

Above: *Wally Hammond – awe-inspiring natural ability*

Hailed at the time of his death as one of the four best batsmen who ever lived, Wally Hammond still numbers among the game's elite, no argument. His athletic frame allowed him to bat and bowl with tremendous power but easy grace, and remain at the top of his game over a long period. Contemporaries were awed by his natural ability and statisticians continue to wonder at his achievements. Hammond first played for England in 1927 and 20 years later, having survived serious illness and the war, he ended his international career with 7249 runs, including 22 centuries, and 85 wickets to his credit. In all first class cricket he scored 50551 runs, including no fewer than 167 hundreds, and claimed 732 wickets. In Ashes cricket he was no less impressive, scoring nine hundreds and regularly sending batsmen packing with his pacy bowling which could, when he was roused, reach frightening speeds. The Australians must have wondered what they had let themselves in for when Hammond first toured down under in 1928/29: his series run total was 905 (at the extraordinary average of 113.12), which included a run of five consecutive innings in which he belaboured the attack for 779. On the Saturday of the 1938 Lord's Test, the largest crowd ever assembled at headquarters watched him complete a masterly 240, at that time the highest score for England in a home Test. Crowds flocked to wherever Hammond played, and he seldom disappointed.

Born: Dover, Kent, 19 June 1903
Died: Kloof, South Africa, 1 July 1965
Roles: Right-hand bat, right-arm fast-medium bowler
Teams: Gloucestershire, England
Ashes debut: 30 November 1928, Brisbane
Last Ashes appearance: 31 January 1947, Adelaide
Ashes appearances: 33
Batting: 2852 runs; average 51.85
Highest score: 251
Bowling: 36 wickets; average 44.77
Best bowling: 5/57
Fielding: 43 caught

Hayward

Below: *Tom Hayward – the best known of a cricketing family*

Tom Hayward was one of the stars of the early struggles for supremacy between England and Australia. Only the second batsman to reach the landmark of 100 first-class centuries after WG Grace, he was acclaimed for his beautiful technique (with his cuts and off drives receiving particular praise), his patience, judgment, watchfulness and strength in defence. No doubt some of his qualities were instilled in him by his father, grandfather and uncle, who all played top class cricket, and they were put to good use when he started playing for Surrey in 1893. His season total of 3518 in 1906 stood as a record until it was beaten by Denis Compton and Bill Edrich in 1947. Hayward's first Test came in South Africa in 1895/96, and his rivalry with the Australian bowlers, which was to encompass three Ashes tours, began soon after. His knock of 130 in the fourth Test at Old Trafford in 1899, begun when England had crumbled to 47 for four, allowed his side to reach a respectable 372 and was described as one of Test cricket's finest. He topped it in the next Test at The Oval by scoring 137, and ended the series with an average of 68.83. While Hayward was never a frontline bowler for England, he was a very useful performer with the ball who could claim the distinction of two hat-tricks in one season, 1899. And throughout his career he was regarded as a model professional who led by example.

Born: Cambridge, 29 March 1871
Died: Cambridge, 19 July 1939
Roles: Right-hand bat, right-arm medium bowler
Teams: Surrey, England
Ashes debut: 22 June 1896, Lord's
Last Ashes appearance: 14 June 1909, Lord's
Ashes appearances: 29
Batting: 1747 runs; average 35.65
Highest score: 137
Bowling: 12 wickets; average 40.50
Best bowling: 4/22
Fielding: 14 caught

Hendren

He was a fine batsman (as good a player as anyone, according to no less an authority than Sir Jack Hobbs), a splendid fielder and catcher in the deep and a great team man, but above all Patsy Hendren was an entertainer. A talented mimic and rapid wit who could have made a living on the stage in the opinion of one contemporary, he could be counted on to liven up proceedings with a joke or a jape whenever the action flagged. This is not to devalue Hendren's contribution to the Middlesex and England causes, however. Averaging 47.63 in his 51 Test matches, he stands behind only Hobbs and Frank Woolley in the list of English top scorers in first-class cricket (with 57,611 runs) and behind only Hobbs in terms of centuries scored (170). Christened Elias Henry but known as Patsy because of his Irish ancestry, he didn't take long to impress the Australians, scoring a half-century in his first Test and following up with 67 in his next innings. Perhaps the pick of his three Ashes centuries came at Brisbane in 1928 when, while hitting 169 in England's first innings, he batted 'superbly, neglecting few opportunities of scoring, running no risk, and driving, cutting and hooking with the utmost certainty', according to Wisden. The innings contributed hugely to an England victory by the huge margin of 675 runs. The man who was born to entertain had put on yet another superb performance.

Above: *Patsy Hendren – a born entertainer*

Born: Turnham Green, London, 5 February 1889
Died: Tooting Bec, London, 4 October 1962
Roles: Right-hand bat, right-arm slow bowler
Teams: Middlesex, England
Ashes debut: 17 December 1920, Sydney
Last Ashes appearance: 29 July 1934, Leeds
Ashes appearances: 28
Batting: 1740 runs; average 39.54
Highest score: 169
Bowling: 1 wicket; average 31.00
Best bowling: 1/27
Fielding: 16 caught

Hobbs

Right: *Jack Hobbs – like Tom Hayward, a Cambridge man*

Far Right & Below: *No one has scored more first-class runs than Hobbs*

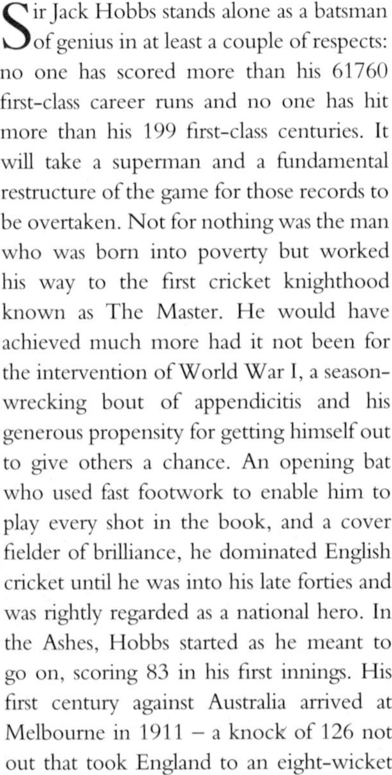

Sir Jack Hobbs stands alone as a batsman of genius in at least a couple of respects: no one has scored more than his 61760 first-class career runs and no one has hit more than his 199 first-class centuries. It will take a superman and a fundamental restructure of the game for those records to be overtaken. Not for nothing was the man who was born into poverty but worked his way to the first cricket knighthood known as The Master. He would have achieved much more had it not been for the intervention of World War I, a season-wrecking bout of appendicitis and his generous propensity for getting himself out to give others a chance. An opening bat who used fast footwork to enable him to play every shot in the book, and a cover fielder of brilliance, he dominated English cricket until he was into his late forties and was rightly regarded as a national hero. In the Ashes, Hobbs started as he meant to go on, scoring 83 in his first innings. His first century against Australia arrived at Melbourne in 1911 – a knock of 126 not out that took England to an eight-wicket win – and it was followed in the next match, at Adelaide, by his highest Ashes score of 187. He was 46 when he compiled his last big innings against the Aussies, 142 at Melbourne in 1929. When at last he retired, he had racked up 12 centuries and 15 fifties in Ashes contests, second only to that other knight, Sir Don Bradman.

Born: Cambridge, 16 December 1882
Died: Hove, East Sussex, 21 December 1963
Roles: Right-hand bat, right-arm medium bowler
Teams: Surrey, England
Ashes debut: 1 January 1908, Melbourne
Last Ashes appearance: 16 August 1930, The Oval
Ashes appearances: 41
Batting: 3636 runs; average 54.26
Highest score: 187
Fielding: 11 caught

Hussain

Right: *Nasser Hussain – helped to lay the foundations of a strong England team*

Remembered as much for his positive, inventive captaincy as for his combative batting style, Nasser Hussain is credited with turning England's fortunes round from 1999 onwards. Unlike Mike Brearley, another imaginative skipper who transformed the national team, his position in the side on batting merit alone was never questioned, and he was even described by Simon Barnes of The Times as 'the most significant cricketer to have played for England since the war'. High praise indeed, and well deserved. Hussain scored 5764 Test runs for England, with 14 centuries among them. He was in charge on the field for 45 of his 96 Tests and won 17 of them, making him the country's fourth most successful captain after Michael Vaughan, Peter May and Brearley. And while his captaincy record in the Ashes – two wins in eight matches – is not as impressive, he had the respect of every single Aussie he faced. His two centuries in Ashes matches included a magnificent 207 at Edgbaston in 1997 that made a mockery of Australia's first-innings collapse and put England on the path to a nine-wicket victory. The other hundred came in very different, trying circumstances at Headingley in the same series, when Australia cruised to an innings win. Hussain scored 11 fifties in the Ashes, the last two coming in his last Test against Australia at Sydney in 2003, when his 75 and 72 and his inspired captaincy helped inflict the hosts' first home defeat in four years. It was not enough to win the Ashes, but Hussain had laid the foundations for glories to come.

Born: Madras, India, 28 March 1968
Roles: Right-hand bat, leg spin bowler
Teams: Essex, England
Ashes debut: 1 July 1993, Nottingham
Last Ashes appearance: 2 January 2003, Sydney
Ashes appearances: 23
Batting: 1581 runs; average 38.56
Highest score: 207
Fielding: 17 caught

Hutton

So intense was the teenage Len Hutton's drive for perfection that experienced coaches examining his technique realised there was nothing that could be improved. When, aged 17, he made his debut for Yorkshire in 1934, he was already the finished article. And so began a first-class career that ended with a knighthood, 40140 runs, 129 centuries, a batting average of 55.51 and the admiration of cricket fans everywhere. In Test cricket, Sir Len won 79 caps, became the first professional to captain England, scored 6971 runs and claimed 19 hundreds at an average of 56.67. He was, simply, one of the best batsmen of any age, as any Australian opponent would confirm. His Ashes cricket began in perfect style when, opening the batting as usual, he scored precisely 100 in his first innings, and at The Oval in the same 1938 series he set the cricket world alight with his Test record-beating 364 as England piled up 903 for seven. Hutton was just 22 at the time. Wisden remarked that 'no more remarkable exhibition of

Left: *Len Hutton – one of the best batsmen of any age*

Born: Pudsey, Yorkshire, 23 June 1916
Died: Kingston-upon-Thames, Surrey, 6 September 1990
Roles: Right-hand bat, leg spin bowler
Teams: Yorkshire, England
Ashes debut: 10 June 1938, Nottingham
Last Ashes appearance: 25 February 1955, Sydney
Ashes appearances: 27
Batting: 2428 runs; average 56.46
Highest score: 364
Bowling: 1 wicket; average 60.00
Best bowling: 1/2
Fielding: 22 caught

HUTTON

Right: *Len Hutton scored a century in his first Ashes innings*

concentration and endurance has ever been seen on the cricket field'. The war intervened, but despite injury and illness Hutton was a long way from being finished. As late as 1953 he was scoring a glorious 145 in the Lord's Ashes Test and by the time his last tour ended he had plundered the Australians for five centuries and 14 fifties. Troubled by ill health, he retired in 1956, shortly after being knighted. The honour has never been more deserved.

Knott

Above: *Alan Knott – perfectionist who always sought to improve*

The sight of Alan Knott stretching, flexing and bouncing between deliveries – as well as whipping out opposing batsmen with a deft stumping or an acrobatic catch – gladdened the hearts of Kent and England cricket supporters for more than 20 years. He was a perfectionist who never ceased to seek out some minor improvement in his technique, and who made sure he was in peak condition to play to his huge potential. Add the fact that he was a gifted bat who scored 17 first-class centuries and 97 fifties and you have the perfect wicketkeeping component of a national team. Knott was seen at his best when he was keeping to the nippy left-arm spinners and in-dippers of his Kent colleague Derek Underwood – if it was tricky facing 'Deadly' as a batsman it was equally so as a keeper, yet Knott seldom let one through. He first played for England in 1967 and made his Ashes debut the following year. At that summer's Headingley Test his first-innings victims included three stumped off the bowling of Ray Illingworth. In 1970/71 he toured down under with Illingworth's team and made a valuable contribution with bat and gloves as the urn returned to English keeping. Perhaps his best innings came at Trent Bridge in 1977, when his 'impudent' 135 set up a seven-wicket England win and the retention of the Ashes. The great series of 1981 saw Knott play in the final two Tests and end his international career with 70 not out at The Oval. It was a fitting end to a wonderful career.

Born: Belvedere, Kent, 9 April 1946
Roles: Right-hand bat, wicketkeeper
Teams: Kent, Tasmania, England
Ashes debut: 6 June 1968, Manchester
Last Ashes appearance: 27 August 1981, The Oval
Ashes appearances: 34
Batting: 1682 runs; average 32.98
Highest score: 135
Fielding: 97 caught, 8 stumped

Right: *Alan Knott was at his best standing up to the wicket*

Laker

Any account of Jim Laker's Ashes career must inevitably focus on the five Old Trafford days in 1956 when he stood the record book on its head. Ian Johnson's tourists had won one and lost one of the three preceding Tests before arriving in Manchester and finding a pitch with which they were far from happy. When they got around to replying to England's 459, they found Laker well-nigh unplayable. His nine wickets for 37 in the first innings and 10 for 53 in the second not only rewrote the records, possibly for all time, they also gave England an innings victory and the series. Laker's 19 for 90 remains the best match bowling analysis in first-class cricket, and it was even more remarkable for the fact that he had already dismissed ten Aussies in an innings that summer, playing for Surrey at The Oval. He had started life as a batsman and fast bowler but switched to finger spin during the war. Together with his Surrey 'spin twin' Tony Lock – who picked up the only wicket not

Left: *Jim Laker – possessor of the best bowling analysis in first-class cricket*

Right:: *Jim Laker is presented with the two balls with which he routed the Australians at Old Trafford in 1956*

Born: Bradford, Yorkshire, 9 February 1922
Died: Putney, London, 23 April 1986
Roles: Right-hand bat, right-arm off spin
Teams: Surrey, Essex, Auckland, England
Ashes debut: 10 June 1948, Nottingham
Last Ashes appearance: 13 February 1959, Melbourne
Ashes appearances: 15
Bowling: 79 wickets; average 18.27
Best bowling: 10/53
Batting: 277 runs; average 14.57
Highest score: 63

snaffled by Laker at Manchester in 1956 – he baffled and irritated a generation of batsmen, ending his Test career with 193 victims and conceding a mere 21.24 runs for each one. Naggingly accurate, he even improved on that average when playing against Australia, and he could often be relied on to hold his end up with some sensible batting. His extraordinary performances will be remembered for ever.

Larwood

Above: *Harold Larwood – a bowler of sometimes terrifying pace*

It is regrettable that Harold Larwood is remembered by some only for his central role in England's notorious Bodyline tour of Australia in 1932/33. There was much more to his game than the fast leg theory, devised by captain Douglas Jardine, that targeted the Australian batsmen with short deliveries aimed at the leg stump, and with a semi-circle of close fielders waiting for leg-side deflections, prods and fendings-off. The Test series, which was won by England 4-1 and which yielded 33 wickets to Larwood at an average of less than 20, provoked enormous controversy as well as serious injuries, but the bowler was forever unrepentant. He was doing no more than following instructions, he insisted, and it should be emphasised that when he emigrated to Australia later in life he was welcomed with genuine warmth. It is sad that following the Bodyline tour Larwood, refusing to apologise, never played for England again. His country thus missed out on several years of a magnificent cricketer who combined terrifying pace – batsmen could often be assured of facing deliveries of between 95 and 100 mph – with uncanny accuracy and a mastery of swing. The former teenage miner played at full tilt, amassing 1427 first-class wickets at 17.51 and gathering more than 7000 runs. But not enough of today's cricket followers know about his devastating display in Brisbane in 1928 when he took six for 32, including a spell of three wickets in five overs for nine runs.

Born: Nuncargate, Nottinghamshire, 14 November 1904
Died: Randwick, New South Wales, 22 July 1995
Roles: Right-hand bat, right-arm fast bowler
Teams: Nottinghamshire, England
Ashes debut: 26 June 1926, Lord's
Last Ashes appearance: 23 February 1933, Sydney
Ashes appearances: 15
Bowling: 64 wickets; average 29.87
Best bowling: 6/32
Batting: 386 runs; average 19.30
Highest score: 98
Fielding: 12 caught

Lilley

Below: *Dick Lilley – outstanding wicketkeeper and batsman*

Dick Lilley was recognised as one of the best wicketkeepers of the early days of international cricket, and his record certainly stands up to the sternest scrutiny. In the 35 Test matches he played against South Africa and Australia, he despatched 92 victims, 22 of them stumped. He was a very useful, forceful batsman as well, scoring 903 in those matches and, according to Wisden, he could 'generally be relied on for runs'. In all first-class matches he scored more than 15000 runs, including 16 centuries, and accounted for 715 batsmen caught and 196 stumped. While performing with distinction behind the stumps against Australia, Lilley also passed the fifty mark on four occasions while batting, the highlight the 84, with 13 fours, he scored at Sydney in 1901. That tour was the first of just two he made of Australia; the second followed in 1903/04, when his performances reached no great heights. It's fair to say Lilley was not the greatest favourite of the cricket establishment of his time, one reason being that he declined to stand up to the wicket to quick bowlers, on the advice of no less a figure than WG Grace. Arguing against tradition and accepted practice was not well regarded in those days. While England captains willingly sought the benefit of his experience and advice, Lilley angered his county captain when he started to set fields behind the skipper's back. His days were numbered.

Born: Birmingham, 28 November 1866
Died: Bristol, 17 November 1929
Role: Right-hand bat, right-arm medium bowler, wicketkeeper
Teams: Warwickshire, England
Ashes debut: 22 June 1896, Lord's
Last Ashes appearance: 9 August 1909, The Oval
Ashes appearances: 32
Batting: 801 runs; average 20.02
Highest score: 84
Bowling: 1 wicket; average 23.00
Best bowling: 1/23
Fielding: 65 caught, 19 stumped

MacLaren

Above: *Archie MacLaren – set a record individual innings score of 424*

One of the true heroes of the game as the 19th century turned into the 20th, Archie MacLaren was an entertainer and a record-breaker who delighted the crowds. Opening the batting for Lancashire at Taunton in 1895 – the summer following his first Ashes tour – he punished the Somerset attack to the tune of 424, including 62 fours. It was a record first-class score that was to stand until Bill Ponsford belted 429 while playing for Victoria against Tasmania in 1923, and it is still the eighth highest score of all time. MacLaren's first-class career brought him 22236 runs in 424 matches, at an average of 34.15, and included 47 hundreds. All of his Tests were played against Australia and he was team captain in 22 of them. He was rather unlucky not to lead the national side to a series victory, but he often felt he was playing under the handicap of having inferior players forced on him by the selectors. To prove his point as late in his career as 1921, when he was nearly 50, he chose 11 amateurs to play Australia at Eastbourne and emerged as the victor by 28 runs. MacLaren's first Ashes century came on his first tour, in 1894/95, when he scored 120 in the fifth Test at Melbourne, and he followed it up with four further hundreds. The last one came at Trent Bridge in 1905 when he drove, pulled and leg glanced his way to 140 in the second innings. The knock was described as nothing short of magnificent.

Born: Whalley Range, Manchester, 1 December 1871
Died: Bracknell, Berkshire, 17 November 1944
Role: Right-hand bat
Teams: Lancashire, England
Ashes debut: 14 December 1894, Sydney
Last Ashes appearance: 9 August 1909, The Oval
Ashes appearances: 35
Batting: 1931 runs; average 33.87
Highest score: 140
Fielding: 29 caught

May

Right: *Peter May (right) – a beautiful batting style and excellent captaincy skills*

From his earliest days at the wicket, Peter May had the look of a future England captain about him. Gifted with a beautiful, classical batting style that brought him big scores from a tender age, he had a manner that exuded quiet, effortless authority. He moved from his private school to Cambridge University, onwards to Surrey and then into the England team as if it were the most natural career progression in the world. Making his Test debut against the South Africans at Headingley in 1951, May promptly made 138 in his first innings, outscoring the great Len Hutton. His best Test innings, 285 not out against the West Indies at Edgbaston in 1957, defying the mysteries of Sonny Ramadhin's spin, is the stuff of legend. In the 1956 series against the Aussies, when not many runs were scored at all, he totalled 453 at an average of 90.60, being dismissed for less than 50 just once. He had been made skipper the previous year and such was his success at the job that England didn't lose under his captaincy until 1958. Of the 41 Test matches with him at the helm, England won 20 and lost just ten; indeed, May's England did not lose a series until the winter of 1958/59, when the wiles of Richie Benaud led the Aussies to a 4-0 win. The leg spinner repeated the trick in 1961, when his team left England with a 2-1 series victory. He was the only captain who managed to defeat May, who retired due to illness that same year.

Born: Reading, Berkshire, 31 December 1929
Died: Liphook, Hampshire, 27 December 1994
Role: Right-hand bat
Teams: Cambridge University, Surrey, England
Ashes debut: 11 June 1953, Nottingham
Last Ashes appearance: 17 August 1961, The Oval
Ashes appearances: 21
Batting: 1566 runs; average 46.05
Highest score: 113
Fielding: 10 caught

Peel

Above: *Bobby Peel – gifted*

There is some debate as to whether Bobby Peel should be regarded as a left-arm spin bowler who was capable with a bat or as a genuine all-rounder who could also boast of being a fine fielder. It doesn't really matter. The fact is he made valuable contributions to both Yorkshire and England with bat and ball and an impression on county and Australian players, the latter over eight Test series and 20 matches. In his 436 first-class matches he scored 12191 runs and captured 1775 wickets, his bowling average of 16.20 testifying to his consistent accuracy and deep understanding of the spinner's art. He maintained his proud record in Tests, all of which were against Australia: he took five wickets in an innings five times, ten in a match once and contributed three fifties with the bat. Peel took 21 wickets in his first three international outings and in the only Test of England's 1888 tour of Australia, at Sydney, claimed nine wickets for the paltry runs-against total of 58. The summer of 1888 also proved to his liking and confirmed that he was deadly given a sticky wicket to bowl on: he took 171 first-class wickets in all, including 24 in three Tests against the Australians at the astonishing average of 7.54. His seven wickets for 31 in Australia's first innings at Old Trafford, followed by four for 37 in the second, was his best haul in Tests.

Born: Churwell, Leeds, 12 February 1857
Died: Morley, Leeds, 12 August 1941
Roles: Left-hand bat, left-arm slow bowler
Teams: Yorkshire, England
Ashes debut: 12 December 1884, Adelaide
Last Ashes appearance: 10 August 1896, The Oval
Ashes appearances: 20
Bowling: 101 wickets; average 16.98
Best bowling: 7/31
Batting: 427 runs; average 14.72
Highest score: 83
Fielding: 17 caught

Pietersen

Below: *Kevin Pietersen – compares favourably to the greatest batsmen in history*

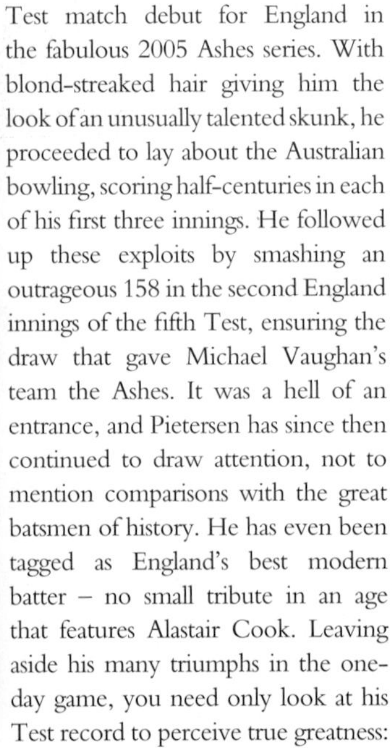

Kevin Pietersen is hard to miss when he is on a cricket field, commanding attention as he does, and you certainly couldn't mistake him when he made his Test match debut for England in the fabulous 2005 Ashes series. With blond-streaked hair giving him the look of an unusually talented skunk, he proceeded to lay about the Australian bowling, scoring half-centuries in each of his first three innings. He followed up these exploits by smashing an outrageous 158 in the second England innings of the fifth Test, ensuring the draw that gave Michael Vaughan's team the Ashes. It was a hell of an entrance, and Pietersen has since then continued to draw attention, not to mention comparisons with the great batsmen of history. He has even been tagged as England's best modern batter – no small tribute in an age that features Alastair Cook. Leaving aside his many triumphs in the one-day game, you need only look at his Test record to perceive true greatness: in advance of the 2013 Ashes he had scored 22 hundreds (three against Australia) and 20 fifties in running up 7,414 runs at an average of 49.42. In the Ashes his average is even better. A large component of his total against Australia came at Adelaide in 2010 when, in a magical performance, he put to bed memories of a failed spell as England captain and hit his way to 227. There is more to come from this phenomenal cricketer.

Born: Pietermaritzburg, South Africa, 27 June 1980
Roles: Right-hand bat, right-arm off spin
Teams: KwaZulu Natal, Nottinghamshire, Hampshire, Royal Challengers Bangalore, Surrey, Deccan Chargers, Delhi Daredevils, England
Ashes debut: 21 July 2005, Lord's
Ashes appearances: 17
Batting: 1476 runs; average 52.71
Highest score: 227
Bowling: 1 wicket; average 141.00
Best bowling: 1/10
Fielding: 9 caught

Rhodes

A young Wilf Rhodes played his first Test match against Australia at Trent Bridge in 1899 and his last against the West Indies at Kingston, Jamaica in 1930, when he was 52. In between, he won a reputation as one of cricket's greatest figures; a wily slow left-arm bowler who used variations in flight as much as spin to winkle batsmen out, and a doughty bat who scored nearly 40000 career runs, with 58 hundreds. Deadly on a sticky wicket, he sent 4204 batsmen packing in his 30-year-plus run in the game, a number that still stands as a record. Rhodes' proficiency with the bat only came after he'd had a few years' practice. He went in at number 11 in his first Test, at Trent Bridge, scoring six in his only innings; in 1903/04, with Tip Foster, he helped to set a record of 130 for the last wicket at Sydney; by the time Melbourne in February 1912 rolled around he was opening the batting with Jack Hobbs and scoring 179. But it is on his bowling that most attention is focused. Rhodes claimed 127 Test wickets, most of them belonging to Australians, with the acme of his Ashes career coming in 1904 at Melbourne, where he failed with the bat but made up for it with the ball. Match figures of 15 for 124 gave England victory by 185 runs and a 3-2 series win. No wonder he went on to become Test cricket's oldest player.

Above: *Wilf Rhodes – lethal on a sticky wicket*

Born: Kirkheaton, Yorkshire, 29 October 1877
Died: Branksome Park, Dorset, 8 July 1973
Roles: Right-hand bat, left-arm slow bowler
Teams: Yorkshire, England
Ashes debut: 1 June 1899, Nottingham
Last Ashes appearance: 14 August 1926
Ashes appearances: 41
Bowling: 109 wickets; average 24.00
Best bowling: 8/68
Batting: 1706 runs; average 31.01
Highest score: 179
Fielding: 36 caught

Snow

Below: *John Snow – had brushes with umpires, cricket authorities and spectators*

A combination of a strong, wilful character, an unwillingness to bow to authority and the kind of injuries that often haunt a fast bowler meant that John Snow gained no more than 49 caps for England. He was unquestionably the country's leading quick bowler from the mid-1960s to the mid-70s, and many a bruised batsman could testify to his pace and hostility. The son of a vicar, Snow first played for England in 1965, and he had several celebrated victims to his name by the time he faced Australia at Old Trafford in 1968. His first go at the Aussie batsmen yielded four wickets and at the end of the series he had claimed 17 wickets. But it was down under in 1970/71 that he really made his mark. Bowling very fast and very aggressively, and despite some suspect umpiring, he forced more than one retirement through injury while taking 31 wickets in the Ashes series and helping England regain the urn. There were brushes with angry spectators, umpires and authorities as Snow, bowling superbly, took seven for 40 in 17.5 overs in the fourth Test at Sydney. Over the course of his Ashes career he helped himself to four five-fors and proved himself no mug with the bat. Overall in Tests he took 202 wickets at an average of 26.66 while in first-class cricket he finished with 1174 dismissals at 22.73. The fact that he sometimes seemed to be bowling well within himself helped to explain the title of his no-punches-pulled autobiography: Cricket Rebel.

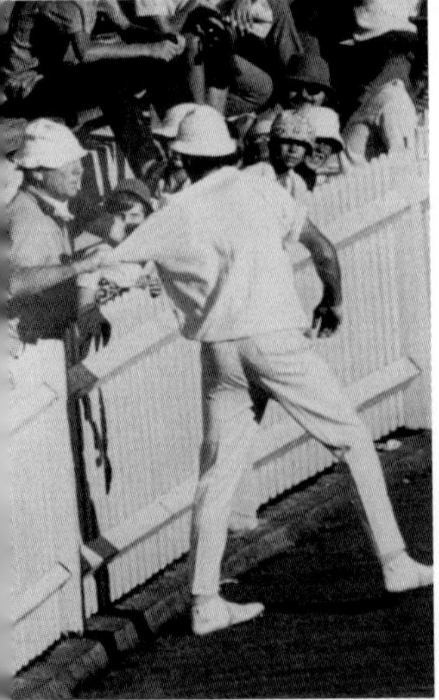

Born: Peopleton, Worcestershire, 13 October 1941
Roles: Right-hand bat, right-arm fast bowler
Teams: Sussex, Warwickshire, England
Ashes debut: 6 June 1968, Manchester
Last Ashes appearance: 28 August 1975, The Oval
Ashes appearances: 20
Bowling: 83 wickets; average 25.61
Best bowling: 7/40
Batting: 392 runs; average 15.07
Highest score: 48
Fielding: 7 caught

Statham

It might sometimes appear that Brian Statham played a subordinate role in the two great fast-bowling partnerships for which he is best known: those with Frank 'Typhoon' Tyson and 'Fiery' Fred Trueman. That impression is false and does an injustice to a bowler who gathered 252 Test match wickets and 2260 in the first-class game, the latter at a miserly average of 16.37. Always annoyingly accurate (from the batter's perspective), he could bowl at genuine pace with complete control over his in-jaggers. Having played his way into his county side on his 20th birthday and made his Test debut the following year, he first played against Australia in 1953 and in the winter of 1954/55 he was on his way to the Antipodes. With the super-speedy Tyson bowling with the wind and Statham plugging away into it, England won the series 3-1 and the Lancashire bowler picked up 18 wickets. Next time out, in 1958/59, he took the first Australian innings apart at Melbourne, finishing with seven for 57. As his partnership with Trueman flourished, the pair toured Australia in 1962/63 with both of them threatening Alec Bedser's England Test record of 236 wickets. It was Statham who broke the record, although Trueman went on to be the first cricketer to smash through the 300-wicket barrier. That was to be Statham's last Ashes encounter, although he did not play his final Test until 1965. He may have been one of the game's gentlemen, but he played second fiddle to no one.

Above: *Brian Statham – nagging accuracy and total control of the ball gave him 69 wickets in the Ashes*

Born: Gorton, Manchester, 17 June 1930
Died: Stockport, Cheshire, 10 June 2000
Roles: Left-hand bat, right-arm fast-medium bowler
Teams: Lancashire, England
Ashes debut: 25 June 1953, Lord's
Last Ashes appearance: 15 February 1963, Sydney
Ashes appearances: 22
Bowling: 69 wickets; average 30.98
Best bowling: 7/57
Batting: 236 runs; average 12.42
Highest score: 36*
Fielding: 11 caught

Stewart

Below: *Alex Stewart – dashing opening bat and diligent wicketkeeper*

Alec Stewart's Test match career proved long, fruitful and record-breaking. No Englishman has won more Test caps than his 133, and few have entertained the crowds as much as the Surrey bat turned wicketkeeper-batsman. Like his father Micky, he was originally thought of purely as a batter; it was when Jack Russell retired in 1998 that Stewart found himself behind the stumps for England on a permanent basis, complementing his invaluable fifties and hundreds, often excitingly compiled, with a good few dismissals. There were many big Test scores – 15 centuries and 45 fifties – among a Test match run total of 8463, to go with 263 catches and 14 stumpings. Against Australia, Stewart was quick off the mark with 79 in the first innings of the Melbourne Test of 1990/91, followed by 91 at Sydney. Although he topped the 100 mark in the Ashes just once – at Melbourne in 1998 – he threatened to do so many more times, and he has 13 fifties to his name. He captained England on 15 occasions, winning on four of them, but his captaincy record against Australia in 1998/99 was mediocre: England lost 3-1. To tell the truth, Stewart seldom showed true skipper qualities. But it's as a dashing opening bat that most will remember him, driving, cutting and pulling his way to 26165 first-class runs at an average of 40.06 and showing particular relish for fast bowling. His last first-class match came, fittingly, at The Oval in 2003 when, to his delight and that of his supporters, England beat South Africa.

Born: Merton, Surrey, 8 April 1963
Roles: Right-hand bat, wicketkeeper
Teams: Surrey, England
Ashes debut: 23 November 1990, Brisbane
Last Ashes appearance: 2 January 2003, Sydney
Ashes appearances: 33
Batting: 1810 runs; average 30.67
Highest score: 107
Fielding: 82 caught, 2 stumped

Sutcliffe

One risks running out of superlatives when describing the talents and career of the great opening batsman Herbert Sutcliffe. A cricketer with immense powers of concentration and doggedness, he was also blessed with the highest degree of natural talent and, to the dismay of bowlers, treated every single ball on its merits: nothing that had gone before, or that threatened to come after, had any effect on the way he faced each delivery. He formed several historic opening partnerships, notably with Jack Hobbs for England and with Percy Holmes and Len Hutton for Yorkshire. And when he had finished, Sutcliffe had scored 50670 first-class runs (including 4555 for England) at an average of 52.02 (an English record 60.73 in Tests) with 151 centuries (16 for England). He first encountered Australian cricketers during the winter of 1924/25, and it was a winter that brought him the wonderful total of 734 runs in five Tests. His batting average was an extraordinary 81.55 and he posted four hundreds and two half-centuries. During the Bodyline series of 1932/33, Sutcliffe notched his highest Test match score of 194 in the first Test at Sydney in spite of playing a Bill O'Reilly delivery on to his stumps – the bails failed to fall. On that tour he was batting without Hobbs, with whom he had formed the perfect partnership, one that is usually considered cricket's best. For an England supporter, nothing was so delightful as watching Hobbs and Sutcliffe playing their team out of trouble on a sticky.

Above: *Herbert Sutcliffe – treated every delivery on its merits*

Born: Harrogate, Yorkshire, 24 November 1894
Died: Cross Hills, Yorkshire, 22 January 1978
Roles: Right-hand bat, right-arm medium bowler
Teams: Yorkshire, England
Ashes debut: 19 December 1924, Sydney
Last Ashes appearance: 18 August 1934, The Oval
Ashes appearances: 27
Batting: 2741 runs; average 66.85
Highest score: 194
Fielding: 15 caught

Tate

Right: *Maurice Tate – batsman and spinner who switched to pace bowling with great success*

As introductions to Test cricket go, it takes some beating. Fast-medium bowler Maurice Tate, picked to play at Edgbaston in 1924, ran in to bowl the second over of South Africa's reply to England's 438 and, first ball, bowled captain Herbie Taylor. Tate and Arthur Gilligan proceeded to mop up the rest of the SA batsmen for 30 and a fabulous Test career was born. The Sussex all-rounder went on to take 2784 first-class wickets at the low average of 18.16 and score 21717 runs at 25.04. In Test cricket he captured 155 wickets, taking five wickets in an innings seven times, and rattled up 1198 runs. But Tate's career is also remarkable in that he was originally considered a batsman first and a spinner second, only switching to pace bowling at Gilligan's insistence, with considerable success. A bowler of ample build, easy rhythm and great stamina, 'Chubby' is credited with being the first to use the seam to obtain movement off the pitch. Against Australia he never managed to hit a hundred but his bowling was definitely not to the Aussies' liking. During the Ashes series of 1924/25 he dismissed 38 of their batsmen at a cost of 23.18 apiece, the highlight being his 11 for 228 in the first Test at Sydney. He 'had exasperating luck in often just missing the stumps,' noted Wisden. Tate was a popular figure whose cheerful demeanour lit up many a cricket ground.

Born: Brighton, Sussex, 30 May 1895
Died: Wadhurst, Sussex, 18 May 1956
Roles: Right-hand bat, right-arm medium-fast, medium and off spin bowler
Teams: Sussex, England
Ashes debut: 19 December 1924, Sydney
Last Ashes appearance: 16 August 1930, The Oval
Ashes appearances: 20
Bowling: 83 wickets; average 30.60
Best bowling: 6/99
Batting: 578 runs; average 19.93
Highest score: 54
Fielding: 7 caught

Taylor

Left: *Bob Taylor – a useful bat and an exemplary wicketkeeper*

There are always arguments, but you can travel a long way before you find anyone to disagree with the theory that Bob Taylor was England's best wicketkeeper of all time. It's safe to say his career record of 1649 dismissals in first-class matches, with 1473 caught and 176 stumped, will never be beaten. His errors were so rare that they were regarded as collector's items. And yet Taylor was for long in the shadow of Alan Knott, the better batsman, when it came to selection for England. He made his Test debut in New Zealand in 1970/71 but it took Knott's defection to World Series Cricket in 1977 for Taylor to gain a well-merited regular place in his country's side. He certainly took his chance well, accounting for 174 batsmen (167 caught, seven stumped) in his 57 Tests before calling it a day. He clearly had an appetite for Ashes cricket, snapping up five victims on his debut at Brisbane in 1978/79 and recording his highest first-class score, 97, in the fifth Test at Adelaide on the same tour. It says much about his character that he walked, not waiting for the umpire's raised finger, three runs short of a hundred as soon as he saw the faintest of leg-side touches nestling in Australian keeper Kevin Wright's gloves. Taylor continued to make useful runs and provide bowlers with the tidiest of services behind the stumps in four further Ashes series up to 1984, when he played his last Test in Pakistan. It was the end of an exemplary career.

Born: Stoke-on-Trent, Staffordshire, 17 July 1941
Roles: Right-hand bat, wicketkeeper
Teams: Derbyshire, England
Ashes debut: 1 December 1978, Brisbane
Last Ashes appearance: 2 January 1983, Sydney
Ashes appearances: 17
Batting: 468 runs; average 17.33
Highest score: 97
Fielding: 54 caught, 3 stumped

Trueman

Right & Below: *Fred Trueman – commentator of long standing after a brilliant fast bowling career*

The cricket world rose to applaud when, on 15 August 1964 at The Oval, the Australian Neil Hawke fell to a slip catch off the bowling of Fred Trueman. Hawke was the Yorkshire fast bowler's 300th Test victim, it was the first time that milestone had been passed and Trueman's eventual tally of 307 wickets stood as a record until beaten by Lance Gibbs in 1976. As it turned out, that Test was also Trueman's last encounter with the Australians, with whom he had enjoyed some terrific tussles. He took five wickets or more in Ashes Tests five times and rarely failed to raise Aussie hackles with his scowling demeanour, extreme pace, hostile approach and fine control of a swinging ball. His international career had begun with a bang in 1952 when, on home ground at Headingley, he helped reduce India's second innings to the

Born: Stainton, Yorkshire, 6 February 1931
Died: Keighley, Yorkshire, 1 July 2006
Roles: Right-hand bat, right-arm fast bowler
Teams: Yorkshire, Derbyshire, England
Ashes debut: 15 August 1953, The Oval
Last Ashes appearance: 13 August 1964, The Oval
Ashes appearances: 19
Bowling: 79 wickets; average 25.30
Best bowling: 6/30
Batting: 338 runs; average 12.07
Highest score: 38
Fielding: 21 caught

Left: *Fred Trueman enjoyed some terrific battles with Australian batsmen*

sorry state of nought for four, taking three of the wickets himself. In the third match of that series he claimed an innings return of eight for 31 and thereafter he terrorised batsman after batsman. His 307 Test wickets came at the exceptional average of 21.57, and let it not be forgotten that Trueman knew one end of a cricket bat from the other. He was also an outstanding fielder, making his name at leg slip. When he retired he was fond of handing out advice to younger players on the BBC's Test Match Special. He had earned that right.

Underwood

Below: *Derek Underwood (right) with John Emburey – heroics at The Oval enabled England to square a series*

'Deadly' Derek Underwood earned his nickname through his performances at a time when England's uncovered pitches allowed him to bowl on a rain-affected track. When conditions favoured his nippy spinners, bowled at a speed many medium-pacers would be happy with, he could be simply unplayable; when they didn't he still picked up wickets through his nagging accuracy and variations in pace and trajectory. The youngest player in the history of the game to reach 100 first-class wickets, he was just 21 when he made his England debut against the West Indies. The proud possessor of 2465 first-class wickets at an average of 20.28 when he retired, Underwood also claimed 297 for England (average 25.83) and took ten wickets in a match six times. Some of his most famous displays came against Australia, and perhaps the most celebrated was the occasion when, on a drying wicket at The Oval in 1968, his four wickets in 27 balls, conceding six runs, gave England a last-gasp win with six minutes of the match remaining. The series was squared and Underwood was a hero. He never matched his seven for 50 in that innings in the Ashes again, but came close when taking six for 45 (ten for 82 in the match) at Headingley in 1972 and seven for 113 (11 for 215 in the match) at Adelaide in 1975. But he was most at home in England's moister conditions, and all of Australia rejoiced when, in 1982, it became clear he had played his last Test.

Born: Bromley, Kent, 8 June 1945
Roles: Right-hand bat, left-arm slow-medium bowler
Teams: Kent, England
Ashes debut: 20 June 1968, Lord's
Last Ashes appearance: 1 February 1980, Melbourne
Ashes appearances: 29
Bowling: 105 wickets, average 26.38
Best bowling: 7/50
Batting: 371 runs; average 12.79
Highest score: 45*
Fielding: 14 caught

Vaughan

Michael Vaughan's career in the Ashes was brief; it was also magnificent. He will be remembered for ever as the man who captained his team in masterful fashion through that incredible series of 2005, when England snatched back the famous little trophy for the first time since 1986/87. He will also be recalled for his marvellous batting against Australia (and every other Test team, for that matter), and for the captaincy skills that made him England's most successful skipper ever: of the 51 Tests between 2003 and 2008 with Vaughan in charge, his team won 26 and lost just 11. He played his first Test cricket in 1999 against South Africa and didn't lock horns with Australia until 2002/03. England were trounced 4-1 but he was named player of the series. And no wonder: he had become the first Englishman for 32 years to score more than 600 in an Ashes series down under, and he had included three centuries in that total. The next set of fixtures against the Aussies was at home in 2005, and you shouldn't need to consult history books to know that England clinched that series 2-1 after the most closely fought, unbearably thrilling Ashes contest ever. Vaughan, naturally, starred with the bat on occasion, making 166 at Old Trafford and 58 at Trent Bridge, but it was mostly his genius for captaincy and his gift for managing men that shone through. That he would never take up the cudgels against Australia again, because of injury, is England cricket's great loss.

Above: *Michael Vaughan – regained the famous urn in 2005 after captaining England in a fabulous Ashes series*

Born: Manchester, 29 October 1974
Roles: Right-hand bat, right-arm off spin
Teams: Yorkshire, England
Ashes debut: 7 November 2002, Brisbane
Last Ashes appearance: 8 September 2005, The Oval
Ashes appearances: 10
Batting: 959 runs; average 47.95
Highest score: 183
Fielding: 2 caught

Right: *Michael Vaughan (centre) was England's most successful skipper*

Verity

His career was tragically short, yet Hedley Verity packed an awful lot into it. His 1956 wickets (not to mention 5603 runs) in 378 first-class matches came at a lowly average of 14.90. He played only 40 Test matches but managed to take five wickets in an innings five times, and ten in a match twice, on his way to a total of 144 dismissals. He was, it's agreed, one of history's best slow left-arm bowlers and one who, with curiosity and humility, never stopped trying to improve his game. Verity had to wait for the retirement of Wilf Rhodes before staking a regular place in the Yorkshire team in 1930, at the age of 25. The following year saw him wearing an England cap for the first time, and he was subsequently chosen for the 1932/33 tour of Australia. Here he was expected to play a supporting role as the fast bowlers carried out their Bodyline attack, but he surprised a few observers by chipping in with a few wickets, including five for 33 at Sydney. When Australia visited England in the summer of 1934, he came into his own; in the second Test at Lord's, a contest known thereafter as Verity's match, he took seven for 61 and eight for 43 as England won by an innings and 38 runs. His last Ashes Test came shortly before the intervention of the war, in which he died a hero's death. England had lost a great man.

Above: *Hedley Verity – a hero*

Born: Leeds, Yorkshire, 18 May 1905
Died: Caserta, Italy, 31 July 1943
Roles: Right-hand bat, left-arm slow bowler
Teams: Yorkshire, England
Ashes debut: 2 December 1932, Sydney
Last Ashes appearance: 20 August 1938, The Oval
Ashes appearances: 18
Bowling: 59 wickets; average 28.06
Best bowling: 8/43
Batting: 344 runs; average 18.10
Highest score: 60*
Fielding: 14 caught

Willis

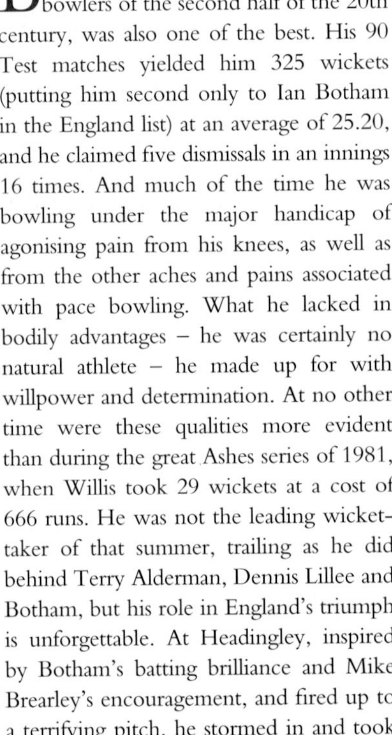

Below: *Bob Willis – bowled his heart out while in constant agonising pain*

Bob Willis, one of England's fastest bowlers of the second half of the 20th century, was also one of the best. His 90 Test matches yielded him 325 wickets (putting him second only to Ian Botham in the England list) at an average of 25.20, and he claimed five dismissals in an innings 16 times. And much of the time he was bowling under the major handicap of agonising pain from his knees, as well as from the other aches and pains associated with pace bowling. What he lacked in bodily advantages – he was certainly no natural athlete – he made up for with willpower and determination. At no other time were these qualities more evident than during the great Ashes series of 1981, when Willis took 29 wickets at a cost of 666 runs. He was not the leading wicket-taker of that summer, trailing as he did behind Terry Alderman, Dennis Lillee and Botham, but his role in England's triumph is unforgettable. At Headingley, inspired by Botham's batting brilliance and Mike Brearley's encouragement, and fired up to a terrifying pitch, he stormed in and took the eight second innings wickets for 43 that shot his side to victory by the margin of 18 runs – one of history's most unimaginable results. It was inevitable that anything following that breathtaking performance would seem ordinary, and Willis chalked up just one further Ashes five-for before bowing to the constant pain and retiring. His next role was the somewhat more knee-friendly one of commentator.

Born: Sunderland, County Durham, 30 May 1949
Roles: Right-hand bat, right-arm fast bowler
Teams: Surrey, Warwickshire, Northern Transvaal, England
Ashes debut: 9 January 1971, Sydney
Last Ashes appearance: 2 January 1983, Sydney
Ashes appearances: 35
Bowling: 128 wickets; average 26.14
Best bowling: 8/43
Batting: 383 runs; average 10.35
Highest score: 26
Fielding: 16 caught

Woolley

Above: *Frank Woolley – a spectators' delight*

Whenever someone compiles a list of the greatest all-rounders cricket has ever had, Frank Woolley is near the top. Often, he leads the list. This was a man who shone in every single department of the game: he scored 58959 first-class runs (average 40.77) with legendary elegance and rapidity; despatched 2066 batsmen (average 19.87) with a graceful bowling action that had spectators purring; and held more catches, 1018, than anyone else in history. In his 64 Test matches he rattled up more than 3000 runs at an average of over 36 and took 83 wickets and 64 catches. Woolley was as effective when playing Australia, against whom he won exactly half of his caps, as against anyone else. He made his Test debut against them in 1909 and three years later was scoring his first Ashes century at Sydney, a beautiful 133 not out that helped England to a 70-run win. When asked to bowl at The Oval in 1912 he dismissed ten Australians for just 49 runs over their two innings to help bring about another convincing victory, by 244 runs. After the Great War he resumed where he had left off, picking up fifties and wickets regularly and recording his second hundred at the Sydney Cricket Ground in 1924. His last Ashes match – his last Test, indeed – did not arrive until 1934, by which time his powers were somewhat diminished. Spectators' memories of one of cricket's greats, however, remained with them for ever.

Born: Tonbridge, Kent, 27 May 1887
Died: Halifax, Canada, 18 October 1978
Roles: Left-hand bat, left-arm medium and slow bowler
Teams: Kent, England
Ashes debut: 9 August 1909, The Oval
Last Ashes appearance: 18 August 1934, The Oval
Ashes appearances: 32
Batting: 1664 runs; average 33.28
Highest score: 133*
Bowling: 43 wickets; average 36.16
Best bowling: 5/20
Fielding: 36 caught

Alderman

Below: *Terry Alderman – his bowling was ideally suited to English conditions*

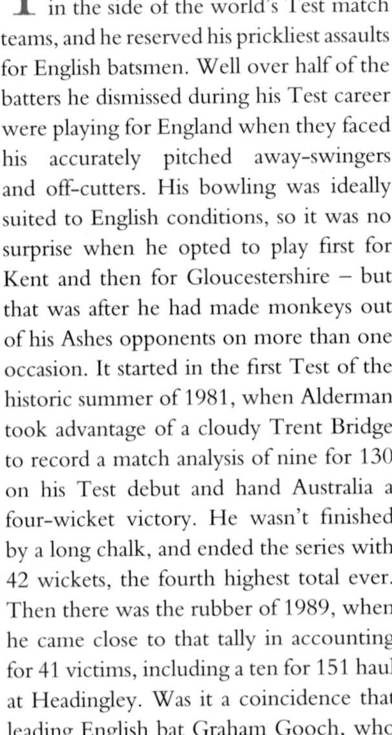

Terry Alderman was a constant thorn in the side of the world's Test match teams, and he reserved his prickliest assaults for English batsmen. Well over half of the batters he dismissed during his Test career were playing for England when they faced his accurately pitched away-swingers and off-cutters. His bowling was ideally suited to English conditions, so it was no surprise when he opted to play first for Kent and then for Gloucestershire – but that was after he had made monkeys out of his Ashes opponents on more than one occasion. It started in the first Test of the historic summer of 1981, when Alderman took advantage of a cloudy Trent Bridge to record a match analysis of nine for 130 on his Test debut and hand Australia a four-wicket victory. He wasn't finished by a long chalk, and ended the series with 42 wickets, the fourth highest total ever. Then there was the rubber of 1989, when he came close to that tally in accounting for 41 victims, including a ten for 151 haul at Headingley. Was it a coincidence that leading English bat Graham Gooch, who was dismissed four times by Alderman in that series, asked to be dropped? Perhaps not. The Western Australian performed very nicely, thank you, in his final Ashes series of 1990/91, taking 16 wickets as the Aussies cruised to a 3-0 win. And that, England's cricketers were happy to note, turned out to be the last time they had to face their bogeyman.

Born: Perth, Western Australia, 12 June 1956
Roles: Right-hand bat, right-arm fast-medium bowler
Teams: Western Australia, Kent, Gloucestershire, Australia
Ashes debut: 18 June 1981, Nottingham
Last Ashes appearance: 1 February 1991, Perth
Ashes appearances: 17
Bowling: 100 wickets; average 21.17
Best bowling: 6/47
Batting: 76 runs; average 9.50
Highest score: 26*
Fielding: 14 caught

Benaud

Above: *Richie Benaud – praised*

As a bowler, Richie Benaud mixed up oppressively accurate leg breaks, topspinners and googlies with the occasional flipper, a potentially deadly variation of the leg spinner's stock deliveries. As a batsman he was watchful yet forceful, looking to get on to the front foot and on top of the bowler. As a fielder he was an agile catcher, excelling at gully or even closer to the wicket. But it was as captain of Australia from the late 1950s to the mid-1960s that he made an enduring mark on the world game. Benaud first played for the side against the West Indies in 1952 and retired in 1964, having taken 248 wickets at 27.03 apiece and scored 2201 runs at the very decent average of 24.45. In between, he helped to transform the Aussies from the underperformers of the early 1950s to world-beaters: of the 28 matches in which he was giving the orders, he won 12 and lost just four. He took on the task of captaincy when Peter May's fancied England side arrived for their 1958/59 tour and promptly trounced them 4-0, taking 31 wickets in the process. He retained the Ashes in 1961, his six wickets for 70 in England's second innings at Old Trafford proving decisive, and he oversaw the 1-1 series draw in 1962/63 that kept the urn in Australian hands. Throughout, his skippering of the side was positive, pragmatic, calculated and inspiring – and the same can be said of his later, much-praised commentary career.

Born: Penrith, New South Wales, 6 October 1930
Roles: Right-hand bat, leg spin bowler
Teams: New South Wales, Australia
Ashes debut: 11 June 1953, Nottingham
Last Ashes appearance: 15 February 1963, Sydney
Ashes appearances: 27
Bowling: 83 wickets; average 31.81
Best bowling: 6/70
Batting: 767 runs; average 19.66
Highest score: 97
Fielding: 32 caught

Right: *Richie Benaud's leg breaks, googlies, topspinners and flippers gave him 83 Ashes wickets*

Boon

Above: *David Boon – many fans' idea of the typical Australian cricketer*

There was a lot more to David Boon's character than the side of him that gave rise to colourful stories of his drinking exploits on long-haul flights, and caused parodists to delight in his luxuriant moustache and rotund appearance. There was, for instance, the side of his personality that took him, often fighting against the odds and always sending fielders sprinting to the boundary, to 21 Test match centuries, 7422 runs, a top score of 200 and an average of 43.65. Boon, whether opening the Australian innings or batting lower down, was indeed a boon to his country. Pugnacious, assertive and indomitable, he represented for many supporters the ideal Aussie cricketer, and he remains Tasmania's favourite player. He played in six Ashes series (four of them won by Australia) and took the English attack for six centuries and seven fifties, coming close to the magical three figures on four occasions. His highest score against the Poms, 184 not out, came at the Bicentenary Test at Sydney in 1988 and was uncharacteristic in its restraint and discipline but completely within character for its match-saving nature. Much more typical was his first hundred on English soil, an innings of 164 not out at Lord's in 1993 that helped to set up an Australian victory by an innings and 62 runs. His last Ashes ton was a knock of 107 at Headingley in the same series. It was his third hundred in successive Tests and left him with a series average of 100.80. After that, it was probably time for a beer.

Born: Launceston, Tasmania, 29 December 1960
Roles: Right-hand bat, right-arm off spin bowler
Teams: Tasmania, Durham, Australia
Ashes debut: 13 June 1985, Leeds
Last Ashes appearance: 3 February 1995, Perth
Ashes appearances: 31
Batting: 2237 runs; average 45.65
Highest score: 164*
Fielding: 25 caught

Border

Right: *Allan Border – vastly influential as skipper of Australia*

Allan Border typified the kind of Australian strength of character and tenacity that have so often subjugated English teams from the 19th century right through to the 21st. A resolute batsman who would sooner surrender all his worldly possessions than his wicket, he squeezed 11174 runs out of the world's Test teams (a national record at the time), scoring 27 hundreds along the way and finishing with an average of 50.56. He was also a tidy left-arm spinner, but it was as captain of the national side – taking over reluctantly from Kim Hughes in 1984 but growing into the job – that he was infinitely more influential. Border skippered the Aussies in 93 Tests, a record number until it was overtaken by South Africa's Graeme Smith, and in all he played 156 Tests, another record of the time. In the Ashes he was a constant irritant to England, compiling eight centuries, passing 50 on 21 occasions and winning 13 of the 29 matches in which he was captain; England won just six. It was in his last

Born: Sydney, New South Wales, 27 July 1955
Roles: Left-hand bat, left-arm slow bowler
Teams: New South Wales, Queensland, Essex, Gloucestershire, Australia
Ashes debut: 29 December 1978, Melbourne
Last Ashes appearance: 19 August 1993, The Oval
Ashes appearances: 47
Batting: 3548 runs; average 56.31
Highest score: 200*
Bowling: 4 wickets; average 93.50
Best bowling: 1/16
Fielding: 57 caught

Ashes series, at Headingley in 1993, that he finally posted a double century against the old enemy. His innings, described by Wisden as 'psychologically brutal', came to an end when he reached the 200 mark and carried on running to the pavilion, declaring the first innings closed at 653 for four. The resulting win enabled a 4-1 series win and Border departed the scene with the Ashes still in Australian hands.

Above: *Allan Border celebrates his world record for the number of Test Match runs*

Bradman

Far Right: *Don Bradman – the greatest batsman of them all*

Below: *Bradman plundered 19 hundreds off the England attack*

There is little you can say about Sir Donald Bradman that hasn't already been said; there are no superlatives that haven't been used; no statistics that haven't been trotted out. He was, simply, the greatest batsman who ever took guard. When he did so for his final Test innings, at The Oval in 1948, he needed a mere four runs to ensure a batting average of 100 at cricket's highest level. To the astonishment of the spectators who had gathered to pay homage, he fell for a second-ball duck. The failure did nothing to diminish the legend, or Bradman's cheerfulness, however; he finished with the average of 99.94, a record that will surely stand for all time. He compiled that average over 80 innings and 20 years, posting 6996 runs and 29 hundreds and all the while humbling every bowling attack. England tried to combat him with the Bodyline plan in 1932/33, and watched as he ran up an average of over 56. Subsequent teams just had to accept that he was too good for them. He played in seven Ashes series and punished the English bowlers to the tune of 19 hundreds, including six doubles and two triples. Of his 334 at Headingley in 1930, the astonishing total of 309 came on the first day, and he went on to score 974 in the series. And the humiliation was to continue for another 18 years. Cricket watched, awed.

Born: Cootamundra, New South Wales, 27 August 1908
Died: Adelaide, South Australia, 25 February 2001
Roles: Right-hand bat, leg spin bowler
Teams: New South Wales, South Australia, Australia
Ashes debut: 30 November 1928, Brisbane
Last Ashes appearance: 14 August 1948, The Oval
Ashes appearances: 37
Batting: 5028 runs; average 89.78
Highest score: 334
Bowling: 1 wicket; average 51.00
Best bowling: 1/23
Fielding: 20 caught

Chappell, Greg

Below: *Greg Chappell – revelled in the chance to take on England*

An elegant batsman who stroked his way to 74 first-class hundreds, Greg Chappell was also a disciplined medium-pace bowler who often captured vital wickets, an outstanding catcher close in and a successful captain – the complete all-rounder, in other words. His total of 87 Test matches would have been higher had he not joined Kerry Packer's breakaway World Series Cricket in 1977, but he still managed to score 7110 Test runs, including 24 centuries, at the excellent average of 53.86 and, on his return to the Australian camp and the captaincy, seal his reputation as the best Australian batsman of his generation. Chappell, like his brothers Ian and Trevor, was a thoughtful player who exuded calm but was capable of rapid scoring when the occasion demanded. He revelled in the chance to take on England, scoring nine hundreds and 12 fifties in seven series and losing just four of the 15 matches in which he captained his team. Among those wins was the Ashes series victory of 1982/83 that followed the shock of the 1981 rubber. His highest Ashes score, an imperious 144 at Sydney in 1975, formed part of a series in which he seldom failed to pass fifty, recording five half-centuries and two hundreds as Australia recaptured the urn. His first ton against England – 108 at Perth in 1970 – had come on his Ashes debut and his last – 115 at Adelaide in 1982 – was achieved in his last series. Greg Chappell was never less than consistent.

Born: Adelaide, South Australia, 7 August 1948
Roles: Right-hand bat, right-arm medium bowler
Teams: Queensland, Somerset, South Australia, Australia
Ashes debut: 11 December 1970, Perth
Last Ashes appearance: 2 January 1983, Sydney
Ashes appearances: 35
Batting: 2619 runs; average 45.94
Highest score: 144
Bowling: 13 wickets; average 52.23
Best bowling: 2/36
Fielding: 61 caught

Chappell, Ian

Above: *Ian Chappell – Australia never lost a series under his captaincy*

The oldest of the Chappell brothers possessed, like his siblings, all the cricket skills necessary to excel at the highest level. Batsman of outstanding efficiency, bowler of leggies that captured 176 first-class wickets and one of an elite group to have claimed 100 Test catches, Ian Chappell was also an innovator and winner as a captain; Australia never lost a series under his leadership. Like his brothers he sometimes sailed close to the wind when it came to matters of sportsmanship, but he was always highly regarded for his knowledge and competitiveness and, in the end, emerged as one of the best captains of any era. Although he did not reach the same batting heights as brother Greg, he nevertheless chalked up 5345 Test runs, with 14 hundreds and 26 fifties, at an average of 42.42. His top score of 196, against Pakistan at Adelaide in 1972, included three sixes in a spell of five balls from Intikhab Alam. As captain in the Ashes between 1971 and 1975 Chappell led his side to seven wins out of 16 matches, and that period witnessed all of the four centuries he posted against England. There were also 15 fifties, for like Greg he was difficult to dislodge once he'd got his eye in. He saved his best for last: the match at The Oval in August 1972 in which he scored an aggressive 192, destined to be drawn in a 1-0 series win for Australia, was his final contest as captain.

Born: Adelaide, South Australia, 26 September 1943
Roles: Right-hand bat, leg spin bowler
Teams: South Australia, Lancashire, Australia
Ashes debut: 28 January 1966, Adelaide
Last Ashes appearance: 1 February 1980, Melbourne
Ashes appearances: 30
Batting: 2138 runs; average 41.11
Highest score: 192
Bowling: 6 wickets; average 71.50
Best bowling: 1/10
Fielding: 31 caught

Clarke

Right: *Michael Clarke – capable of exciting crowds with assured shotmaking*

There is still some way to go in Michael Clarke's Test match career, but his position as one of his country's leading players is already assured. From his current exalted position as captain of his country, with 21 matches and 12 victories under his belt, he can look back on a life in the game that has brought him almost 7000 Test runs compiled at an average of 52.54, with 22 hundreds among the total. Once a batter of unbridled exuberance, he reined in his game to suit the demands of the five-day format but he is still supremely capable of exciting the crowds with his assured shotmaking and knack of finding the holes in a field. Clarke did not take long to make an impression in Ashes cricket, knocking off 91 runs in only 106 balls in his first match at Lord's in 2005 and helping to bring about an Aussie victory by 239 runs. His first century against England came at Adelaide in 2006, in another win for Australia, and it has been followed by three others, including a magnificent 136 at Lord's in 2009 that at one point looked as if it might avert an inevitable defeat. As recently as November 2012 Clarke was scoring 230 against South Africa at Adelaide, one of four double centuries he notched in that year. They included his highest score, a rampaging knock of 329 not out made at Sydney against a shell-shocked India. At 31, Clarke is still one for the future.

Born: Liverpool, New South Wales, 2 April 1981
Roles: Right-hand bat, left-arm slow bowler
Teams: New South Wales, Hampshire, Australia
Ashes debut: 21 July 2005, Lord's
Ashes appearances: 20
Batting: 1365 runs; average 45.50
Highest score: 136
Bowling: 1 wicket; average 147.00
Best bowling: 1/12
Fielding: 15 caught

Davidson

Above: *Alan Davidson – accurate*

Grateful spectators purred with pleasure as they watched Alan Davidson's approach to the wicket and his smooth bowling action; they went into raptures as he hit out powerfully and straight with the bat, sending the ball far over the boundary; and they applauded as he snapped up yet another brilliant catch from close in, or whipped in a deadly accurate return from the outfield. Davidson had everything, but it was as a highly accurate bowler with devastatingly late outswing that he was best known: he picked up 186 wickets, at 20.53 each, in Test cricket and 672 in all first-class matches at pretty much the same average. No surprise that, with Pakistan's Wasim Akram, he is regarded as one of the two best left-arm dealers of pace in the game's history. Making his Test debut against England at Trent Bridge in 1953, Davidson took some time to record his first innings haul of five wickets or more in Ashes cricket, but then it was a superb return of six for 64 at Melbourne in 1959, followed by three more in the second innings, that paved the way for an Aussie win. Four more five-fors were to follow before England saw the last of him. While never registering a Test century, he certainly made a contribution to the cause with five fifties, three scores in the 70s coming in the Ashes. With Richie Benaud he helped to move Australia from the unaccustomed status of also-rans to the position of world leaders.

Born: Gosford, New South Wales, 14 June 1929
Roles: Left-hand bat, left-arm fast-medium bowler
Teams: New South Wales, Australia
Ashes debut: 11 June 1953, Nottingham
Last Ashes appearance: 15 February 1963, Sydney
Ashes appearances: 25
Batting: 750 runs; average 24.19
Highest score: 77*
Bowling: 84 wickets; average 23.76
Best bowling: 6/64
Fielding: 27 caught

Gilchrist

Below: *Adam Gilchrist – a great competitor who 'just hit the ball'*

The first time Adam Gilchrist lined up against England in a Test match, at Edgbaston in July 2001, he bludgeoned his way to 152, and 110 of those runs came from fours and sixes. Next time out, at Lord's, he made another rip-roaring 90. His next innings, at Trent Bridge, brought him a mere 54, but it was from only 59 balls. And so it went on, the England attack often proving powerless to counter this most powerful and exhilarating of wicketkeeper-batsmen. Even in Gilchrist's last Ashes innings, at Sydney in 2007, he notched a thrillingly accrued 62. At Perth earlier in that series, perhaps stung by a first-innings duck, he had hurtled, with 12 fours and four sixes, to 102 in 59 deliveries, the second fastest century in Test history. But England weren't the only team to feel the rough edge of Gilchrist's bat: he marked up 5570 Test runs in his 96 matches, with 17 hundreds, 26 fifties and a top score of 204 not out leaving him with an average of 47.60. And we haven't even talked yet about his wicketkeeping, which made him the leading Australian Test performer of all time: 379 catches and 37 stumpings put him ahead of Ian Healy (who played more matches) and Rod Marsh (who played the same number). Rather tall for a stumper, he nevertheless distinguished himself when keeping to the bowling of Shane Warne – no easy task. Gilchrist, in short, was a one-off, a carefree bloke and great competitor who lived according to his motto: just hit the ball.

Born: Bellingen, New South Wales, 14 November 1971
Roles: Left-hand bat, wicketkeeper
Teams: New South Wales, Western Australia, Middlesex, Australia
Ashes debut: 5 July 2001, Birmingham
Last Ashes appearance: 2 January 2007, Sydney
Ashes appearances: 20
Batting: 1083 runs; average 45.12
Highest score: 152
Fielding: 89 caught, 7 stumped

Gregory

Even the most specialised of batsmen usually develop a little bowling sideline, perhaps dreaming of a hat-trick at Lord's some day. So dedicated to the art and science of batting was Syd Gregory that in his record-breaking 58 Test matches against England he bowled a mere 30 balls, which were despatched for 33 runs. He no doubt shrugged and returned to his batting, which was one of the highlights of the early days of England-Australia encounters. One of the extensive Gregory cricket dynasty that encompassed his father, an uncle, a brother, a brother-in-law and a cousin, he played in 369 first-class matches and hit 15188 runs, 25 hundreds and 65 half-centuries among them. Remarkably, he occupied every one of the 11 batting positions during his Test career. He played nearly all his Test cricket against England, appearing just half a dozen times against South Africa, and it was against the old country that he excelled: every one of his four Test centuries was scored in Ashes matches. The first came at Sydney during England's 1894/95 tour when, batting at six, he scored a wonderful 201 and was doubtless gratified to receive the substantial sum of £103, the result of a collection made at the ground. The last, a second-innings knock of 112 described by Wisden as brilliant, was at the Adelaide Oval in 1904 and it allowed the Aussies to claim victory by 216 runs. There was no collection that time, but the Australian public no doubt expressed their gratitude in other ways.

Above: *Syd Gregory – dedicated to his art*

Born: Sydney, New South Wales, 14 April 1870
Died: Sydney, New South Wales, 1 August 1929
Role: Right-hand bat; right-arm bowler
Teams: New South Wales, Australia
Ashes debut: 21 June 1890, Lord's
Last Ashes appearance: 19 August 1912, The Oval
Ashes appearances: 52
Batting: 2193 runs; average 25.80
Highest score: 201
Fielding: 24 caught

Grimmett

Right: *Clarrie Grimmett – credited with the invention of the flipper*

It's not a bad way to start your life in Test cricket: playing for Australia in the Fifth Test against England in 1925, debutant Clarrie Grimmett spun his way to match figures of 11 wickets for 82, doing more than anyone to ensure an Aussie win by 307 runs. Wisden was mightily impressed, noting that Australia hardly needed to call on the services of the New Zealand-born bowler's fellow leg spinner Arthur Mailey. Grimmett was 33 at the time but he continued to haunt England until he was 42, frustrating batsmen with his accuracy and mystifying them with his mix of leg breaks, topspinners, wrong'uns and flippers – he was credited with the invention of the last-named delivery. His 37-match Test career yielded 216 victims (nearly half of them Englishmen) at an average of 24.21, and he took five wickets in an innings an astonishing 21 times. Such was his impact that he was the first bowler to top the 200-wicket barrier in Tests, and he is still the only one to reach that milestone in fewer than 40 matches. In Ashes cricket there were 11 five-fors, including one in his final appearance against England in 1934. That match, in which Australia's two-innings total was 1028, resulted in the massive winning margin of 562, to which Grimmett contributed with eight for 167. Wisden, as it had been at the beginning, was full of praise. 'Grimmett,' it noted simply, 'bowled superbly.'

Born: Dunedin, New Zealand, 25 December 1891
Died: Adelaide, South Australia, 2 May 1980
Roles: Right-hand bat, leg spin bowler
Teams: Wellington, Victoria, South Australia, Australia
Ashes debut: 27 February 1925, Sydney
Last Ashes appearance: 18 August 1934, The Oval
Ashes appearances: 22
Batting: 366 runs; average 13.07
Highest score: 50
Bowling: 106 wickets; average 32.44
Best bowling: 6/37
Fielding: 7 caught

Grout

Above: *Wally Grout – never on the losing side in a Test series*

Such was the form of rival wicketkeeper Don Tallon that Wally Grout couldn't even claim a regular place in the Queensland team for many years, and he was 30 before he played Test cricket. He made up for lost time at both levels, however, and ended up as one of Australia's best-known and top-performing keepers. After retiring he could look back on a career in which his country never lost a series when he was behind the stumps. In all, 187 victims, including 24 stumped, came his way and he was the first man to catch six batsmen in one innings, setting the record on his Test debut against South Africa in 1957. Grout, an agile keeper who was nicknamed The Voice because of his chatty nature, claimed 17 victims in his first Ashes series, most of them coming from catches off the seam bowlers. His first five-victim haul in an England innings came at Lord's in 1961, when the pace bowling of Graham McKenzie and Frank Misson proved fruitful. The second and last was at Sydney in 1966, during his final Ashes series, and all but one of them were off the bowling of Neil Hawke. He proved his worth as a batsman on more than one Ashes occasion, notably at Melbourne in 1959 when he hooked his way to 74. Grout's rapid-fire wit shone when he was asked if he had attended public school. 'Eton,' came the reply, 'and drinkin'.' He was much missed when a heart attack claimed him early.

Born: Mackay, Queensland, 30 March 1927
Died: Brisbane, Queensland, 9 November 1968
Roles: Right-hand bat, wicketkeeper
Teams: Queensland, Australia
Ashes debut: 5 December 1958, Brisbane
Last Ashes appearance: 11 February 1966, Melbourne
Ashes appearances: 22
Batting: 301 runs; average 13.68
Highest score: 74
Fielding: 69 caught, 7 stumped

Harvey

Below: *Neil Harvey – put England to the sword in 1948*

Neil Harvey was wonderful to watch: a stylish, destructive left-hander with all the shots who loved nothing better than advancing far down the wicket to take on the spinners but who treated the quicks with equal disdain. He would pounce on every opportunity to score – which, in his book, was just about every ball – and scorers were invariably busy with their pencils when he was around. Harvey, the leading Australian batsman of his generation, finished his first-class career with 67 centuries and 94 half-centuries, with 21 and 24 of them, respectively, coming in Test matches. Short in stature, he was nevertheless an athletic fielder of supreme talent and could turn his arm over to good effect, but his batting was naturally to the fore as he started his Test career with the remarkable total of six centuries in his first 13 innings. One of them came on his Ashes debut at Headingley in 1948 when, aged just 19, he put the England attack to the sword in scoring 112 with 17 boundaries. English bowlers were to suffer at Harvey's hands to the tune of five more hundreds before he retired. His highest Ashes score, a knock of 167 in the second Test at Melbourne on England's 1958/59 tour, was achieved with a little more difficulty, but it enabled the Australians to win by eight wickets. He kept his high standards up right to the end, his last hundred against England coming in the fourth Test at Adelaide in 1963 with the end of his Test career just one match away.

Born: Melbourne, Victoria, 8 October 1928
Roles: Left-hand bat, right-arm off spin bowler
Teams: Victoria, New South Wales, Australia
Ashes debut: 22 July 1948, Leeds
Last Ashes appearance: 15 February 1963, Sydney
Ashes appearances: 37
Batting: 2416 runs; average 38.34
Highest score: 167
Fielding: 25 caught

Hassett

Above: *Lindsay Hassett – very high scores were a speciality*

Lindsay Hassett's Test cricket began and ended with Ashes matches. In between there were distinct phases to his progress in the game: the pre-war shotmaker; the more cautious post-war batter; the victorious captain who, ultimately, oversaw the loss of the Ashes after a long period of Australian dominance. In all phases, however, he was capable of very high scoring, and he retired with a first-class batting average of 58.24 to his name, with 59 hundreds and 75 half-centuries contributing to a run total of 16890. In Tests he totalled 3073 runs (average 46.56) with ten centuries. At first his nimble footwork and elegant stroke play brought him runs at a rapid rate, but his more sedate approach following the war was typified by his performance in the first Test at Brisbane in 1946/47: his first-innings 128, his first Ashes century, took over six and a half hours. Slow it might sometimes have been, but Hassett's batting was also mightily effective, and it was no surprise when he succeeded Don Bradman as Test captain in 1949. He excelled in this role, guiding Australia to 14 victories and only four losses during his 24-match tenure. Meanwhile, the big scores continued to accumulate. Despite a Hassett half-century in the final Ashes Test of the summer of 1953 at The Oval, however, Len Hutton's England won the day by eight wickets and the Ashes in the process. The great man thereupon retired to look back on a career in which his teams had bested England many times.

Born: Geelong, Victoria, 28 August 1913
Died: Bateman's Bay, New South Wales, 16 June 1993
Roles: Right-hand bat, right-arm medium bowler
Teams: Victoria, Australia
Ashes debut: 10 June 1938, Nottingham
Last Ashes appearance: 15 August 1953, The Oval
Ashes appearances: 24
Batting: 1572 runs; average 38.34
Highest score: 137
Fielding: 16 caught

Hayden

Right: *Matthew Hayden – his batting could be brutal*

A devout Catholic, Matthew Hayden habitually crossed himself whenever he reached three figures at the batting crease. During the course of an 18-year career in first-class cricket he crossed himself many, many times. The scorer of 79 tons, including 30 in Tests, with the outstanding average of 52.57 (50.73 in Tests), also had much crossing to do in October 2003, when he broke Brian Lara's record for the highest individual Test innings by thrashing the Zimbabwe bowlers for 380 despite suffering from a bad back. It was a typical Hayden innings in its brutality and contempt for the attack; he relied on his immense strength to counteract what some saw as technical deficiencies, driving and sweeping his way to 8625 runs in his 103 Tests. Five centuries came against England, and in one Ashes Test, at his home ground of Brisbane in the winter of 2002/03, he treated the delighted crowd to a lovely double: 197 in the first innings and 103 in the second. England were already soundly beaten before they crumbled to the second-innings 79 that handed Australia victory by 384 runs. That match formed part of a purple patch that saw Hayden punch out six centuries in seven Tests on home territory. In the 2006/07 Ashes series, as Australia waltzed to their 5-0 win, he was eventually as punishing as any of their batters despite a slow start, scoring 92 at Perth and 153 in the Boxing Day Test at Melbourne. That was to be the final time he crossed England, and himself, in Ashes cricket.

Born: Kingaroy, Queensland, 29 October 1971
Roles: Left-hand bat, right-arm medium bowler
Teams: Queensland, Hampshire, Northamptonshire, Australia
Ashes debut: 5 July 2001, Birmingham
Last Ashes appearance: 2 January 2007, Sydney
Ashes appearances: 20
Batting: 1461 runs; average 45.65
Highest score: 197
Fielding: 29 caught

Healy

For what seemed like decades but was actually a mere seven years, Shane Warne and Ian Healy combined to form one of cricket's deadliest duos. It seemed almost every ball delivered by the great leg spinner would be met with an appreciative Healy comment, conveyed to the watching television audience through a stump mic. Too often for the batsman's liking there would be the clatter or thump of ball hitting stumps, pads or wicketkeeping gloves, followed by Healy's roar of delight. He was one of the best Australian keepers of all time and a player who typified the fighting spirit and dedication of the country's teams of the 1990s. He first appeared for Australia's Test team against Pakistan in 1988 having played in just six first-class matches, and worked hard to stay at the top. His Test career total of 366 catches and 29 stumpings was a world record until beaten by his successor, Adam Gilchrist, and then Mark Boucher. As a lower-order bat he carved out 4356 priceless runs at an average of 27.39, with a top score of 161 not out. Healy shone against England, scoring two centuries and snapping up five victims or more in an innings six times. It was during the first Test of the summer of 1997 at Edgbaston that he pouched an Australian record-equalling six catches in England's first innings, mostly off the pace bowlers. His sole victim off Warne's bowling ended Nasser Hussain's knock of 207, and you can bet your bottom Aussie dollar that by the end Hussain was a little tired of hearing from behind him the constant refrain: 'Bowling, Warnie.'

Above: *Ian Healy – formed deadly partnerships with several Australian bowlers*

Born: Brisbane, Queensland, 30 April 1964
Roles: Right-hand bat, wicketkeeper
Teams: Queensland, Australia
Ashes debut: 8 June 1989, Leeds
Last Ashes appearance: 2 January 1999, Sydney
Ashes appearances: 33
Batting: 1269 runs; average 30.95
Highest score: 134
Fielding: 123 caught, 12 stumped

Hill

Right: *Clem Hill – a nightmare for all bowlers*

No batting record was safe when Clem Hill was around. In 1893, aged just 16, he compiled an innings of 360 in a college game in Adelaide, the highest recorded in the country at that time. He exceeded that score while batting for South Australia against New South Wales in 1900/01, hitting 365 and setting a Sheffield Shield record that stood for 27 years. In the following calendar year he scored more than 1000 runs in Test cricket, a feat that would not be matched for 45 years. And when he left Test cricket in 1912 he did so with 3412 runs – more than any other batsman. It was a record that stood for 24 years, and it took a batter of the calibre of Jack Hobbs to beat it. Hill must have loomed large in the nightmares of English bowlers. Standing crouched at the crease before cutting, clipping and driving his way to four centuries in Ashes matches, he also passed 50 on 16 occasions, with five of those innings ending when he was in the 90s. Remarkably, three 90-plus scores came in successive innings, at Melbourne and Adelaide in 1902. But perhaps Hill's best innings was seen at Melbourne in 1898. Australia's first innings stood at 58 for six when he took charge; the next wicket fell at 223, Hill scored a magnificent 188, Australia's innings amounted to 323 and England were beaten by eight wickets. His Test career ended in acrimony following a punch-up with a selector, but his batting record shone through the cloud.

Born: Adelaide, South Australia, 18 March 1877
Died: Melbourne, Victoria, 5 September 1945
Roles: Left-hand bat, right-arm leg spin bowler
Teams: South Australia, Australia
Ashes debut: 22 June 1896, Lord's
Last Ashes appearance: 23 February 1912, Sydney
Ashes appearances: 41
Batting: 2660 runs; average 35.46
Highest score: 188
Fielding: 30 caught

Hogg

Rodney Hogg's time at the forefront of the Australian bowling attack was brief, but it could hardly have been more noticeable. At the age of 27 he stepped into the breach left by the 1977 desertion of Australia's top fast bowlers to World Series Cricket, and he left the scene seven years later having decided to go on 'rebel tours' himself. In that time he accounted for 123 Test batsmen, claiming five wickets in an innings six times and ending with a bowling average of 28.47. But the Ashes stage was the one on which he put on his best performances, and they started with a bang. Steaming in to bowl very fast at an England line-up that boasted the talents of Graham Gooch, David Gower, Ian Botham, Derek Randall et al at Brisbane in 1978/79, he kicked off his Test career with Gooch's wicket and finished his first Test stint with the figures of six for 74. Bruised by England's victory in that match, he raised his game and took ten wickets for 122 in the next one, at Perth. Even better followed at Melbourne, where he finished with ten English scalps for a paltry 66 runs. And so it went on until Hogg had completed the six-match Ashes series with 41 victims at just 12.85 apiece. It must have hurt that England won that series 5-1, so he carried on firing his bullets at Poms until he was banned for his 'rebel' activities. There was seldom a fierier Aussie.

Above: *Rodney Hogg – 56 English wickets at a low average*

Born: Melbourne, Victoria, 5 March 1951
Roles: Right-hand bat, right-arm fast bowler
Teams: South Australia, Victoria, Australia
Ashes debut: 1 December 1978, Brisbane
Last Ashes appearance: 2 January 1983, Sydney
Ashes appearances: 11
Batting: 121 runs; average 7.56
Highest score: 36
Bowling: 56 wickets; average 17.00
Best bowling: 6/74
Fielding: 1 caught

Hughes

Below: *Merv Hughes – big of heart, equally big of moustache*

Merv Hughes' introduction to Ashes cricket was in some ways just as spectacular as that of Rodney Hogg. Playing in only the second Test match of his life at Brisbane in 1986, he found himself bowling at an Ian Botham who was in particularly warlike mood. As Botham clinched a first-innings century he decided to celebrate by taking Hughes to the cleaners, clubbing him for 22 in an over.

But the big-hearted Hughes, refusing to get disheartened, went on to build a career that gave him 212 Test wickets at an average of 28.38. Sometimes called on to bowl lengthy, strength-sapping spells in discouraging circumstances, he never once flagged or failed to find the funny side to a situation. His antics and extensive moustache, which would not have looked out of place on a 19th century bushranger, kept the spectators entertained, and he was a huge crowd favourite wherever he played. Hughes could have been born for Ashes cricket and he bowled at Englishmen with relish, often picking up three or four wickets in an innings but only crossing the five-for barrier once. That was in the first innings of the Trent Bridge Test of 1994, and it was typical of the man that, putting everything into a bouncer in an effort to get rid of centurion Graham Gooch in England's second innings, he strained a groin muscle and played no further part in the match. He bust a gut, you might say.

Born: Euroa, Victoria, 23 November 1961
Roles: Right-hand bat, right-arm fast bowler
Teams: Victoria, Essex, Australian Capital Territory, Australia
Ashes debut: 14 November 1986, Brisbane
Last Ashes appearance: 19 August 1993, The Oval
Ashes appearances: 20
Batting: 278 runs; average 13.23
Highest score: 71
Bowling: 75 wickets; average 30.25
Best bowling: 5/92
Fielding: 5 caught

Langer

At first, Justin Langer's Test career stuttered. Following his debut against the West Indies in 1993 he was in and out of the Australian team despite putting together a reasonable run of scores (and falling for the occasional duck). In six years he played in just eight Tests. But when he got going he blossomed into one of the finest stroke-players seen in the Aussie baggy green. And when he got together with Matthew Hayden at the top of the batting order during the 2001 Ashes series he became part of the second best opening partnership ever – only the Windies' Gordon Greenidge and Desmond Haynes scored more runs together. Langer totalled 7696 Test runs at an average of 45.27, passing the hundred mark on 23 occasions and three times exceeding 200. He never did England any great favours, hitting five centuries in Ashes matches and proving one of their sterner opponents in the memorable 2005 series. In 1998 he ground his way to a knock of 179 not out, followed by 52 in the second innings, that facilitated a 250-run victory. Cudgelling a massive 250 at Melbourne in 2002, he laid the foundations for a five-wicket Australian win that put the icing on the cake of a 4-1 series victory. Like every other right-thinking Aussie, he was desperate to make amends in 2006/07 after losing the Ashes the previous year, and he started off with 82 and 100 not out in the first Test at Brisbane. Once the urn had been regained he regarded his job as done and called it a day.

Above: *Justin Langer – one of Australia's finest stroke-players*

Born: Perth, Western Australia, 21 November 1970
Roles: Left-hand bat, left-arm medium bowler
Teams: Western Australia, Middlesex, Somerset, Australia
Ashes debut: 20 November 1998, Brisbane
Last Ashes appearance: 2 January 2007, Sydney
Ashes appearances: 21
Batting: 1658 runs; average 50.24
Highest score: 250
Fielding: 14 caught

Lawry

Below: *Bill Lawry (left) with Ray Illingworth – stripped his batting back to the essentials*

Many a Test attack foundered on the rock that was Bill Lawry. Long of nose and steady of bat, he was capable of occupying the crease for what could seem like weeks, grinding the bowlers down until they surrendered. At the end of his Test career – which came when he was sacked in 1971, in one of the Australian authorities' most shameful actions; they did not bother to inform him of their decision – he had amassed 5234 runs, with 13 hundreds, at an average of 47.15. Lawry, opening the batting, had formed the rigid backbone of the team on so many occasions that cricket didn't seem quite right without him. Yet he had seemed such a bright young thing when he was introduced to Test cricket on the 1961 Ashes tour of England: starting with a 57 at Edgbaston that was studded with six boundaries, he progressed with a magnificent, chanceless 130 at Lord's as Australia won by five wickets and followed up with innings of 74 and 102 at Old Trafford that helped bring about another victory, by 54 runs. Thereafter he stripped his batting back to the essentials and contented himself with defying every bowling attack on the planet, while scoring plenty of runs. Five more hundreds and 11 fifties followed against England, one of the latter being an 81 at Old Trafford that celebrated the occasion of his first Ashes Test as captain. Lawry skippered the Australians in 25 Tests, winning nine and losing eight of them. The selectors, just like countless bowlers, had to resort to jiggery-pokery to dislodge him.

Born: Melbourne, Victoria, 11 February 1937
Roles: Left-hand bat, left-arm medium bowler
Teams: Victoria, Australia
Ashes debut: 8 June 1961, Birmingham
Last Ashes appearance: 29 January 1971, Adelaide
Ashes appearances: 29
Batting: 2233 runs; average 48.54
Highest score: 166
Fielding: 16 caught

Lawson

Left: *Geoff Lawson – turned to coaching after a famous fast-bowling career*

Some of the batsmen who faced Geoff Lawson, a qualified optometrist, must have wished they had better vision as the bouncers fizzed past their noses. As a young man playing in an England-New South Wales game in 1978/79 he let a few loose at Geoff Boycott, an act that boosted his reputation no end. Soon he was in and about the Australian Test team, but it wasn't until he faced England at Lord's in 1981, in only his third Test, that he made a real impact. His seven for 81 in England's first innings, which included the wickets of the first four batters, put the efforts of Dennis Lillee and Terry Alderman in the shade and ensured a lengthy stint in the side. Lawson, using a combination of hostile pace, bounce and swing, went on to take 180 Test wickets at 30.56 each, with 11 five-wicket and two ten-wicket hauls among the total. More than half of his victims were English. During England's 1982/83 Ashes tour he went on the rampage, collecting 34 victims during the series and picking up four five-fors in the process. His match figures of 11 for 134 in the second Test at Brisbane hustled Australia to a seven-wicket win and gave Bob Willis's men a taste of what was to come. Lawson was nobody's fool with the bat, either: he passed 50 three times in Ashes matches, and his 74 at Lord's in 1989 was rightly praised. England hadn't seen that coming.

Born: Wagga Wagga, New South Wales, 7 December 1957
Roles: Right-hand bat, right-arm fast bowler
Teams: New South Wales, Lancashire, Australia
Ashes debut: 18 June 1981, Nottingham
Last Ashes appearance: 24 August 1989, The Oval
Ashes appearances: 21
Bowling: 97 wickets; average 28.48
Best bowling: 7/81
Batting: 383 runs; average 15.95
Highest score: 74
Fielding: 4 caught

Lillee

Right: *Dennis Lillee – one of cricket's greatest bowlers and possessor of a classic action*

There have been few more awe-inspiring sights in cricket than that of Dennis Lillee's smoothly flowing run-up (often accompanied by raucous chants of 'Lillee, Lillee'), culminating in a soaring leap and a magnificent side-on delivery that sent the ball speeding to its target. The delivery was very often followed by a blood-curdling, finger-pointing appeal and the upward thrust of an umpire's finger. Lillee took 355 Test wickets (average: 23.92) during his career, putting him at the top of the bowling tree at the time, and he is acknowledged as one of the greatest bowlers in cricket's history. At first he terrorised batsmen with sheer speed but as time went on he was forced by injuries to temper his attack. No matter; he was still rapid and could call on the full armoury of the fast bowler's weapons. He had it all, and when you put him up against England, especially when he combined with someone like Jeff Thomson, there were bound to be fireworks. Dismissing five Englishmen

Born: Perth, Western Australia, 18 July 1949
Roles: Right-hand bat, right-arm fast bowler
Teams: Western Australia, Tasmania, Northamptonshire, Australia
Ashes debut: 29 January 1971, Adelaide
Last Ashes appearance: 12 November 1982, Perth
Ashes appearances: 29
Bowling: 167 wickets; average 21.00
Best bowling: 7/89
Batting: 469 runs; average 18.03
Highest score: 73*
Fielding: 6 caught

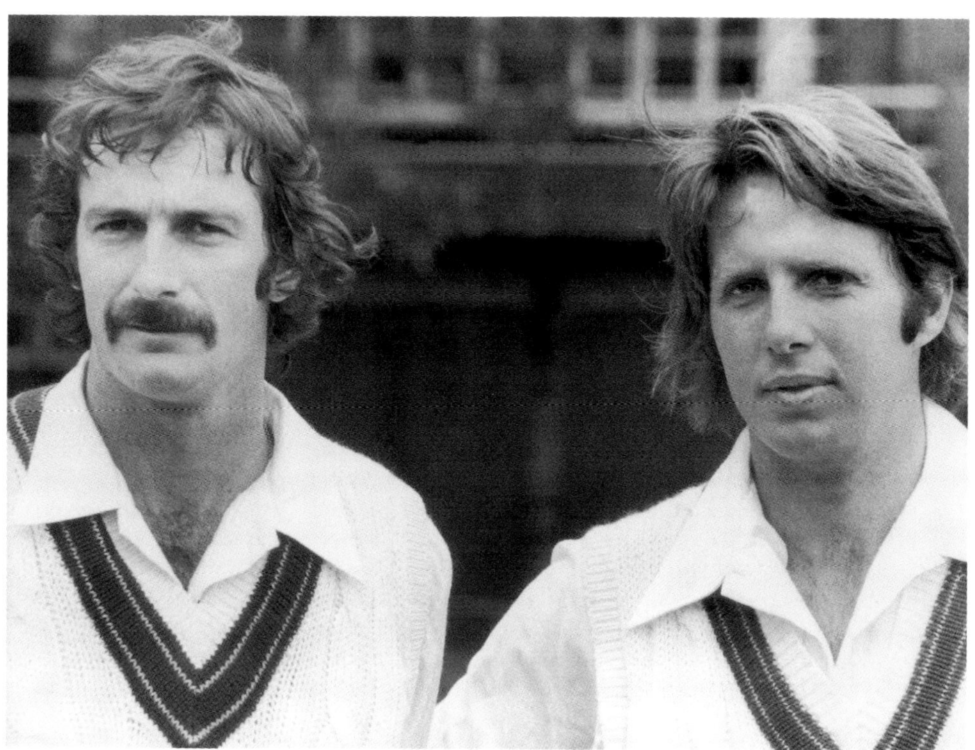

in his first dash at them, at Brisbane in 1971, he ended up taking five or more in an Ashes innings 11 times. Funnily enough, his best figures against the Poms came in his penultimate Ashes match: at The Oval in the tumultuous summer of 1981 he sliced through their first innings (seven for 89) and did what he could in the second (four for 70) as the match fizzled out. He left the Ashes stage a fulfilled and immensely popular man wherever he had played cricket.

Left: *Dennis Lillee (left) formed a deadly fast-bowling partnership with Jeff Thomson*

Lindwall

Far Right: *Ray Lindwall (right) with Richie Benaud – bowled at hair-raising pace*

Below: *Half of Lindwall's Test victims were English batsmen*

Many of the truly great fast bowlers have had the benefit of a pacy partner to share the load and help get the sparks flying. So it was with Ray Lindwall, whose alliance with Keith Miller was rightly feared for ten years in the 40s and 50s. It didn't sound right to say 'Lindwall' without adding 'and Miller'. But he represented a terrific threat to batsmen whether bowling in tandem with the Victorian all-rounder or not. Hair-raising pace, devastating late outswingers, devilish yorkers, and bouncers that threatened to decapitate were just some of the weapons that took Lindwall to 228 wickets, at the average of 23.03, in his 61 Tests. Exactly half of those wickets belonged to English batsmen, against whom the former rugby league player often played at the very top of his game. His best innings figures in an Ashes match of seven for 63 came in only his fourth Test against England, at Sydney in 1947. The following summer he led the way as the Australian 'Invincibles' toured England, 86 wickets tumbling to a man at the peak of his powers. Lindwall saw 27 English batsmen off during that year's Ashes series, and no performance was more widely lauded than his demolition act at The Oval: his six for 20 reduced England's first innings to a sorry 52 all out. Also a lusty swinger of a bat who hit two Test centuries, he was one of the 20th century's most feared purveyors of cricket excellence.

Born: Sydney, New South Wales, 3 October 1921
Died: Brisbane, Queensland, 23 June 1996
Roles: Right-hand bat, right-arm fast bowler
Teams: New South Wales, Queensland, Australia
Ashes debut: 29 November 1946, Brisbane
Last Ashes appearance: 13 February 1959, Melbourne
Ashes appearances: 29
Bowling: 114 wickets; average 22.44
Best bowling: 7/63
Batting: 795 runs; average 22.08
Highest score: 100
Fielding: 17 caught

Macartney

Below: *Charlie Macartney – 'an individual genius'*

Accounts of Charlie Macartney's qualities as a batsman invariably stress his quirky individuality. Wisden noted that he was a law unto himself – 'an individual genius, but not in any way to be copied. He constantly did things that would be quite wrong for an ordinary batsman, but by success justified all his audacities.' And what success this brilliant cricketer achieved. In the 35 Test matches he played in a career disrupted by the Great War and illness he ran up 2131 runs at an average of 41.78, passing the hundred mark seven times. It must not be forgotten that Macartney was also a left-arm spinner of high renown who in his early years was better known for that art than for his batting; at Headingley in July 1909 he took seven for 58 and four for 27 as Australia won by 126 runs. But it was his batting that attracted the eye, and after the war he laid about English bowling with inventive abandon. In 1921 he battered the Nottinghamshire attack for a breathtaking 345, scored in less than four hours, and his final Ashes tour in 1926 featured tons in three successive Tests, at Lord's, Headingley and Old Trafford. Wisden went into raptures in describing the second of the three, an innings of 151 that offered a sumptuous array of drives, cuts and leg-side shots. It was, said the almanack, one of the most glorious displays of a great career.

Born: Maitland, New South Wales, 27 June 1886
Died: Sydney, New South Wales, 9 September 1958
Roles: Right-hand bat, left-arm slow bowler
Teams: New South Wales, Otago, Australia
Ashes debut: 13 December 1907, Sydney
Last Ashes appearance: 14 August 1926, The Oval
Ashes appearances: 26
Batting: 1640 runs; average 43.15
Highest score: 170
Bowling: 33 wickets; average 27.51
Best bowling: 7/58
Fielding: 11 caught

Mailey

Arthur Mailey only played 21 Test matches, but to say that his impact was considerable is to understate the case. He was capable of spinning the ball a long way, and his leg breaks and googlies sent 99 batsmen on the long trudge back to the pavilion during that short international career. Eighteen of those 21 matches were played against England, against whom Mailey shone brightly. On the MCC Ashes tour of 1920/21 led by Johnny Douglas, he nabbed 36 wickets at a cost of 946 runs despite drawing a blank in the second Test at Melbourne. That total included his greatest achievement in Test cricket, a nine for 121 haul in England's second innings in the fourth match (also at Melbourne) that remains Australia's best performance. Mailey was on a roll and, having sailed to England the following summer with Warwick Armstrong's side, he took the country by storm. The tour saw him snap up 146 wickets in all matches at an average of 19.61, and they included the ten he took for 66 against Gloucestershire. His second tour, in 1926, yielded him a further 141 dismissals. Mailey went out on a high, spinning his way to a match return of nine for 266 in his final Test, at The Oval in 1926. His first three wickets on that occasion, all clean bowled, were those of Jack Hobbs, Herbert Sutcliffe and Frank Woolley – not a bad note on which to end.

Above: *Arthur Mailey – capable of spinning the ball a long way*

Born: Sydney, New South Wales, 3 January 1886
Died: Sydney, New South Wales, 31 December 1967
Roles: Right-hand bat, leg spin bowler
Teams: New South Wales, Australia
Ashes debut: 17 December 1920, Sydney
Last Ashes appearance: 14 August 1926, The Oval
Ashes appearances: 18
Bowling: 86 wickets; average 34.12
Best bowling: 9/121
Batting: 201 runs; average 11.82
Highest score: 46*
Fielding: 12 caught

Marsh

Right: *Rod Marsh, loser of a bet with Mike Gatting (left) – record-setting wicketkeeper*

The solid figure cut by Rod Marsh as he stood behind the stumps belied his agility, nimble feet and speedy glove work. These, together with razor-sharp reflexes, occasional acrobatics and a wonderful dedication to his work, brought him 355 Test match victims – a record at the time. And coincidental as it may be that Dennis Lillee finished with the same number of wickets, the two men forged a partnership that has never been matched: the entry 'c Marsh b Lillee' appeared 95 times on Test scorecards. Marsh was also a splendid, combative batsman who notched three Test centuries and 16 fifties, often coming together with Lillee to shore up the Australian lower order. Against England he made one century and nine half-centuries, and twice came within a few shots of three figures; his aggressive 91 at Old Trafford in 1972 was likened to an innings from the great hitter Gilbert Jessop. Even so, it was his wicketkeeping that attracted most plaudits for Marsh. At Brisbane in 1982 he claimed six victims in an Ashes innings, equalling Wally Grout's Australian record and facilitating a seven-wicket victory, and he contributed to five dismissals in an innings twice more. It was in that 1982/83 series that he set a Test match record that still stands despite the efforts of the likes of Ian Healy and Adam Gilchrist. Marsh caught 28 English batsmen that winter, almost all of them off the bowling of the Australian pacemen. His working relationship with Lillee came to an end at that time, as did the Ashes career of a very fine cricketer.

Born: Perth, Western Australia, 4 November 1947
Roles: Left-hand bat, wicketkeeper
Teams: Western Australia, Australia
Ashes debut: 27 November 1970, Brisbane
Last Ashes appearance: 2 January 1983, Sydney
Ashes appearances: 42
Batting: 1633 runs; average 27.21
Highest score: 110*
Fielding: 141 caught, 7 stumped

Massie

A few cricketers featured in this book had brief but spectacular Ashes careers. None were as brief as that of Bob Massie, and very few were as spectacular. Massie's Test star burned fiercely for a few days in June 1972; thereafter it sparkled once or twice before crashing into the Caribbean Sea. The bewhiskered swing bowler won a place in the Australian side that toured England in 1972 on the strength of decent performances against a Rest of the World team and his experience of league cricket in Scotland. Limbering up with six wickets for 31 against Worcestershire, he was called up to make his Test debut in the second Ashes match at Lord's. And what a debut it was. Under heavy skies, Massie bowled unrelentingly accurately and with late swing both ways, bewitching and bewildering his opponents until he had taken eight wickets for 84 and England were out for 272. Then, after Australia had accumulated 308, he put on an even better show in grabbing eight for 53 as England were skittled for 116. His match figures of 16 for 137 were at the time the best by a Test debutant and are still the best ever by an Australian at any career stage. But that, more or less, was that for Massie. His first-class career began to fizzle, and it went out on a tour of the West Indies when he lost the knack of swinging a ball. He only played in six Tests. Stranger things might have happened at sea, but not in the Test match arena.

Above: *Bob Massie – applauded from the field after his amazing Ashes debut at Lord's*

Born: Perth, Western Australia, 14 April 1947
Roles: Left-hand bat, right-arm medium-fast bowler
Teams: Western Australia, Australia
Ashes debut: 22 June 1972, Lord's
Last Ashes appearance: 10 August 1972, The Oval
Ashes appearances: 4
Bowling: 23 wickets; average 17.78
Best bowling: 8/53
Batting: 22 runs; average 4.40
Highest score: 18

McCabe

Below: *Stan McCabe – extraordinary courage and aggression*

When a cricketer of the heroic stature of Sir Donald Bradman describes an innings as the greatest example of batting he ever saw, you know he is talking about a batsman of precious talent. The Don had witnessed at first hand a historic knock of 232 by Stan McCabe, one of the Australians who were replying to an England first innings of 658 in the first Test of 1938 at Trent Bridge. For four hours, as the Aussies fought to avoid the follow-on, McCabe took the attack to England, raising the temperature of his assault as the end neared. Wisden was ecstatic about his 'merciless punishment of the bowling' and doubted whether the innings' equal had ever been seen. Perhaps it didn't come as much of a surprise to those who had watched the Bodyline series of 1932/33. McCabe defied the vicious bowling of Larwood and Voce with extraordinary courage and aggression in those Tests, hooking his way to 385 runs. They included a lion-hearted unbeaten knock of 187, out of an Australian total of 278, at Sydney. In all Tests he made 2748 runs, including six hundreds, at an average of 48.21, and he also bagged 36 wickets with his medium-pace off-cutters. In the Ashes he piled up four centuries and ten fifties, all the while displaying a brilliant technique that many thought superior to Bradman's. Stan McCabe was a bowler's nightmare but a spectator's dream.

Born: Grenfell, New South Wales, 16 July 1910
Died: Sydney, New South Wales, 25 August 1968
Roles: Right-hand bat, right-arm medium bowler
Teams: New South Wales, Australia
Ashes debut: 13 June 1930, Nottingham
Last Ashes appearance: 20 August 1938, The Oval
Ashes appearances: 24
Batting: 1931 runs; average 48.27
Highest score: 232
Bowling: 21 wickets; average 51.23
Best bowling: 4/41
Fielding: 21 caught

McGrath

The top three wicket-takers in Test match history – Muttiah Muralitharan, Shane Warne and Anil Kumble – were all spinners of one sort or another. Next comes Glenn McGrath, Test cricket's most successful quick bowler with the enormous total of 563 wickets to his credit, amassed in fewer matches than the top trio and taken at a more economical rate. McGrath was a bowling phenomenon, his gangly six feet five inch frame able to extract bounce from wickets where others found none, and his pitiless accuracy exasperating countless batters. To these attributes he added the ability to move the ball off the seam and in the air, a nice line in sledging and the propensity to win his mind games with opponents, making the complete bowling package. No wonder he is thought of as Australia's best paceman after Dennis Lillee. McGrath's best innings return in Tests was the eight for 24 with which he bulldozed Pakistan at Perth in 2004, and his eight for 38 against England at Lord's in 1997 was scarcely inferior. That performance came in his first Test in England, and was followed later in the summer by a seven-for-76 at The Oval that gave him 36 wickets in the series. Naturally, some of his best bowling was reserved for Ashes matches; he chalked up five wickets or more in an England innings ten times. Having dismissed 21 Englishmen in the whitewash of 2006/07 he deemed the job done and retired with full legendary status.

Above: *Glenn McGrath – 500 Test wickets won him golden boots*

Born: Dubbo, New South Wales, 9 February 1970
Roles: Right-hand bat, right-arm fast-medium bowler
Teams: New South Wales, Worcestershire, Middlesex, Australia
Ashes debut: 25 November 1994, Brisbane
Last Ashes appearance: 2 January 2007, Sydney
Ashes appearances: 30
Bowling: 157 wickets; average 20.92
Best bowling: 8/38
Batting: 105 runs; average 6.17
Highest score: 20*
Fielding: 10 caught

McKenzie

Below: *Graham McKenzie – smooth approach, explosive delivery*

As a young man Graham McKenzie wielded a bat to good effect and turned a mean off break. It wasn't long after he lengthened his run-up and took to bowling at a rapid clip that it became clear Australia had found yet another exceptional pace bowler. Making his Test debut on his first Ashes tour, at Lord's in 1961 – and dismissing five Poms in the second innings to mark the occasion – 'Garth' went on to capture 246 wickets at the highest level. That put him, in career terms, just two behind the man who gave him his Test chance, Richie Benaud, but ahead of any other Australian at the time. He overcame the five-wickets-in-an-innings barrier 16 times and took ten wickets in a match on three occasions. Such was his impact that when he surged past 200 Test wickets against the West Indies in 1968/69, he was the youngest man to reach that milestone. Not the most rapid of quicks, McKenzie was nevertheless a constant source of bother for English batsmen, his smooth approach being followed by explosive but controlled deliveries that offered a consistent threat. His seven for 153 at Old Trafford in 1964, taken as England replied to Bobby Simpson's first-innings 311 with 611 runs of their own, is remembered as a triumph for persistence and skill, while his six for 48 at Adelaide in 1966 was a match-winner. The fast bowler's life, rewarding but often painful, proved too onerous in the end, and McKenzie left the Test scene to bowl superbly for Leicestershire.

Born: Perth, Western Australia, 24 June 1941
Roles: Right-hand bat, right-arm fast bowler
Teams: Western Australia, Leicestershire, Australia
Ashes debut: 22 June 1961, Lord's
Last Ashes appearance: 9 January 1971, Sydney
Ashes appearances: 25
Bowling: 96 wickets; average 31.34
Best bowling: 7/153
Batting: 252 runs; average 9.33
Highest score: 34
Fielding: 11 caught

Miller

Never one to waste time, Keith Miller introduced himself to Ashes cricket with a match-winning performance with bat and ball. In the first Test of the 1946/47 season at Brisbane he smote 79 runs as Australia ran up 645 in their only innings. Then, following a ferocious thunderstorm, he sliced through the England batting, taking seven wickets for 60 and, when the tourists followed on, a further two before letting Ernie Toshack finish the job. Australia won by an innings and a lot of runs following a typical performance from a man whom the Aussies look on as their greatest all-rounder. A stylish, powerful bat, a fiery, improvisatory purveyor of high pace (often in tandem with Ray Lindwall) and a magnificent slip catcher, he also endeared himself to the Australian public with a refreshingly non-conformist attitude to the game and to life. Miller hit 2958 runs (average: 36.97) and took 170 wickets (22.97) in his 55 Test matches and, as is often the case with Australians, he reserved many of his finest feats for the Ashes. He scored three centuries and took five wickets in an innings three times against England, two of the latter returns coming in one match at Lord's in 1956, when his match analysis of ten for 152 helped Australia to victory by 185 runs. Praise came from every quarter, and Sir Len Hutton summed up his inimitable style when he called Miller the most unpredictable cricketer he had played against.

Above: *Keith Miller – inimitable, unpredictable*

Born: Melbourne, Victoria, 28 November 1919
Died: Melbourne, Victoria, 11 October 2004
Roles: Right-hand bat, right-arm fast bowler
Teams: Victoria, New South Wales, Nottinghamshire, Australia
Ashes debut: 29 November 1946, Brisbane
Last Ashes appearance: 23 August 1956, The Oval
Ashes appearances: 29
Batting: 1511 runs; average 33.57
Highest score: 145*
Bowling: 87 wickets; average 22.40
Best bowling: 7/60
Fielding: 20 caught

Morris

Below: *Arthur Morris – rapid accumulator of runs*

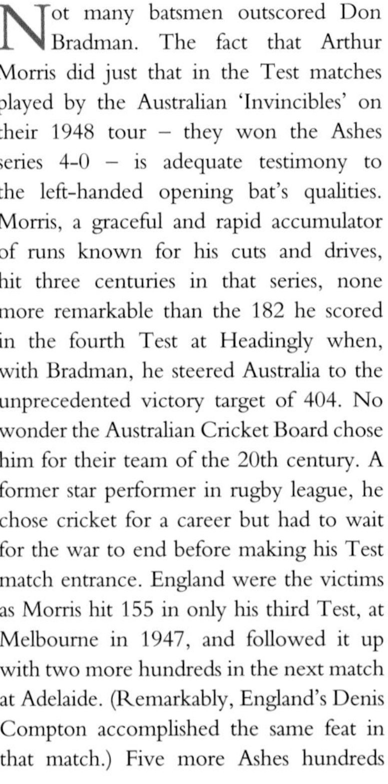

Not many batsmen outscored Don Bradman. The fact that Arthur Morris did just that in the Test matches played by the Australian 'Invincibles' on their 1948 tour – they won the Ashes series 4-0 – is adequate testimony to the left-handed opening bat's qualities. Morris, a graceful and rapid accumulator of runs known for his cuts and drives, hit three centuries in that series, none more remarkable than the 182 he scored in the fourth Test at Headingly when, with Bradman, he steered Australia to the unprecedented victory target of 404. No wonder the Australian Cricket Board chose him for their team of the 20th century. A former star performer in rugby league, he chose cricket for a career but had to wait for the war to end before making his Test match entrance. England were the victims as Morris hit 155 in only his third Test, at Melbourne in 1947, and followed it up with two more hundreds in the next match at Adelaide. (Remarkably, England's Denis Compton accomplished the same feat in that match.) Five more Ashes hundreds were to follow, the highest coming at Adelaide again in 1951, when he battled back from uncertainty against his bête noire Alec Bedser to finish in sparkling form with 206 to his name. Morris scored 3533 runs at an average of 46.48 in all Tests, marking up 12 centuries and the same number of fifties. Sadly, his form waned as he moved into his 30s, but the memories of a masterful batsman remained.

Born: Sydney, New South Wales, 19 January 1922
Roles: Left-hand bat, left-arm chinaman bowler
Teams: New South Wales, Australia
Ashes debut: 29 November 1946, Brisbane
Last Ashes appearance: 28 January 1955, Adelaide
Ashes appearances: 24
Batting: 2080 runs; average 50.73
Highest score: 206
Bowling: 1 wicket; average 39.00
Best bowling: 1/5
Fielding: 9 caught

O'Reilly

Bill O'Reilly was English batsmen's nemesis so often during the 1930s that they must have longed for his early retirement. In the end it was the war that ended the torment, but it didn't come before he had captured five English wickets in an innings eight times and ten wickets in a match on three occasions. O'Reilly, who was on the tall side for a spinner, sent down his leg breaks, topspinners and googlies at a brisk pace, disguising each delivery so effectively that he was almost impossible to pick. He combined those attributes with a warlike attitude to become one of the finest bowlers ever to grace the game. Donald Bradman, who didn't always see eye to eye with O'Reilly, nonetheless called him the best there had ever been. Eight out of every ten of his 144 Test wickets (taken at an average of 22.59) were those of Englishmen. He made his Ashes debut at Sydney in 1932 and in the very next Test, at Melbourne, he baffled the Poms so much that he ended the match with ten wickets at less than 13 runs apiece. He struck 27 times in that Bodyline series, which was won 4-1 by England, and that was the last time the enemy tasted victory in O'Reilly's time. In his penultimate Ashes match, at Headingley in 1938, he claimed ten dismissals once again as Australia won by five wickets. And then the man they accurately called Tiger finally left England alone.

Above: *'Tiger' O'Reilly – combative attitude*

Born: White Cliffs, New South Wales, 20 December 1905
Died: Sydney, New South Wales, 6 October 1992
Roles: Left-hand bat, leg spin bowler
Teams: New South Wales, Australia
Ashes debut: 2 December 1932, Sydney
Last Ashes appearance: 20 August 1938, The Oval
Ashes appearances: 19
Bowling: 102 wickets; average 25.36
Best bowling: 7/54
Batting: 277 runs; average 10.65
Highest score: 42
Fielding: 4 caught

Ponsford

Right: *Bill Ponsford – born to beat records*

Only two cricketers have scored 400 runs or more in a first-class innings on two occasions. One is the world-beating Trinidadian Brian Lara; the other was the doughty opening batsman Bill Ponsford, a man who seemed to be born to beat records, often at England's expense. He bettered the mark for the best individual score twice with those 400-plus innings and he still holds, with Don Bradman, the record for the highest Australian partnership in Test cricket. That stand of 451, for the second wicket of the Aussies' first innings at The Oval in 1934, included a glorious 266 by Ponsford, but it heralded the end of his Test career. If he had a weakness it was fast, hostile bowling, and the fearful battering he took during the Bodyline tour of 1932/33 – he estimated he had been hit by Larwood and Voce 50 times during the three Tests he played – seemed to take its toll of his reserved character. But Ponsford had already made a huge mark on Test cricket, and he scored 2122 runs at an average of 48.22, racking up seven hundreds, during a ten-year career. His first Test innings, against England at Sydney in 1924, was a knock of 110 and he followed it up with 128 in the next match. The centuries (five of them) and fifties (five more) kept coming, each accrued with the use of a Big Bertha, a massive bat that he could wield dextrously thanks to his enormous forearm strength. His untimely retirement was a great loss to cricket.

Born: Melbourne, Victoria, 19 October 1900
Died: Kyneton, Victoria, 6 April 1991
Roles: Right-hand bat, right-arm medium bowler
Teams: Victoria, Australia
Ashes debut: 19 December 1924, Sydney
Last Ashes appearance: 18 August 1934, The Oval
Ashes appearances: 20
Batting: 1558 runs; average 47.21
Highest score: 266
Fielding: 17 caught

Ponting

There is a very strong case to be made for the theory that Ricky Ponting was among the two or three most important cricketers ever to play for Australia. He scored more Test runs (13378) and centuries (41) than any of his compatriots, having earned 168 caps, a record he shares with Steve Waugh. As captain he oversaw 44 Test victories, more than any other man, and lost just 16 of his 77 matches in charge. He shared another distinction with Waugh: a peerless run of 16 Test wins. He also holds the Australian Test records for most centuries (seven in 2005) and most runs (1544 in 2006) in a calendar year. Ponting's intensely competitive nature, allied to supreme batting prowess and superb catching skills, made him one of the greatest. You would be hard pressed to disagree once you had witnessed him at work, pulling, hooking and cover driving his way to yet another big score or calling the shots in the field. Yet his record in the Ashes was blemished by three series defeats – a record of which England can be immensely proud. Ponting, on the other hand, punished his Ashes opponents with the bat, chalking up eight centuries and nine fifties, with many innings of matchless beauty among them. The first ton came in his maiden Ashes Test at Headingley in 1997; the last came at Cardiff 13 years later. The latter innings, a knock of 150 that touched perfection, took him through the 11,000 Test run barrier – yet another milestone for Punter.

Above: *Ricky Ponting – one of Australia's greatest cricketers*

Born: Launceston, Tasmania, 19 December 1974
Roles: Right-hand bat, right-arm medium bowler
Teams: Tasmania, Somerset, Australia
Ashes debut: 24 July 1997, Leeds
Last Ashes appearance: 26 December 2010, Melbourne
Ashes appearances: 35
Batting: 2476 runs; average 44.21
Highest score: 196
Bowling: 1 wicket; average 27.00
Best bowling: 1/9
Fielding: 41 caught

Simpson

Right: *Bobby Simpson – technical excellence and remarkable concentration took him to massive scores*

Bobby Simpson was, it seems, never satisfied with a mere century against England; he had to go on to higher things. The first time he made it into three figures in an Ashes match, at Old Trafford in 1964, he went on and … and on … for nearly 13 hours, finally being dismissed when he had 311 on the scoreboard. The next and final time, at Adelaide in 1966, he didn't stop until he had compiled a commanding 225 and put Australia on the way to an innings victory. A purist in terms of technique, Simpson was noted for his thoroughness in preparation and his mighty powers of concentration. They served him well throughout his 62 Test matches, in which he scored 4869 runs at an average of 46.81 and claimed 71 wickets at 42.26. He was also a slip fielder of the highest class who snaffled 110 Test catches, a skilful bowler and a capable skipper who claimed 12 wins and 15 draws in his 39 matches at the helm. Against England he took some time to get fully into his batting stride – as in his overall Test career, in which he had to wait until his 30th Test for a ton – but finished with nine Ashes half-centuries to go with those massive scores. England players came to dread the moments when he and Bill Lawry clattered down the pavilion steps to open an Australian innings. They knew it might be a very long time before either of them retraced their steps.

Born: Sydney, New South Wales, 3 February 1936
Roles: Right-hand bat, leg spin bowler
Teams: New South Wales, Western Australia, Australia
Ashes debut: 31 December 1958, Melbourne
Last Ashes appearance: 11 February 1966, Melbourne
Ashes appearances: 19
Batting: 1405 runs; average 50.17
Highest score: 311
Bowling: 16 wickets; average 52.37
Best bowling: 5/57
Fielding: 30 caught

Slater

Left: *Michael Slater (in discussion with umpire Venkataraghavan) – a favourite among Australian supporters*

Michael Slater's bold approach to batting, the game of cricket and life in general made him many friends on both sides of the Ashes divide, although the English had good cause to curse him. He made a deep impression on the old rivalry, and at the end of his last match in 2001 he had hit seven Ashes centuries out of a total of 14 in all Tests. He had entered the five-day arena against England in 1993, just a few months after forcing his way into the New South Wales team, and his spectacular style soon made him a favourite among Aussie supporters. Slater's debut at Old Trafford, opening alongside fellow Wagga Wagga man Mark Taylor, saw him ease away from the starting gate with a nice half-century, and it was followed in the next match at Lord's by a thrilling 152 as Australia won by an innings. At Brisbane the following winter he started in marvellous style, compiling a first-innings 176 from only 244 balls, cracking 25 boundaries along the way. He had the bit between his teeth by now and he continued to punish England, adding three half-centuries to his tally before he was done. In all Tests Slater ran up a total of 5312 runs at an average of 42.83, becoming known meanwhile for sometimes failing to convert 90s into tons. His last Ashes century came in 1999 at Sydney, where his second-innings 123 out of an Australian total of 184 pushed them towards a 98-run victory. His batting deteriorated somewhat after that, but it had been an exhilarating ride.

Born: Wagga Wagga, New South Wales, 21 February 1970
Roles: Right-hand bat, right-arm medium bowler
Teams: New South Wales, Derbyshire, Australia
Ashes debut: 3 June 1993, Manchester
Last Ashes appearance: 16 August 2001, Leeds
Ashes appearances: 20
Batting: 1669 runs; average 45.10
Highest score: 176
Fielding: 8 caught

Spofforth

Right: *Fred Spofforth (front, left) – transformed his bowling and reaped rich rewards*

Apparently self-dubbed the Demon Bowler, Frederick Spofforth was one of the leading lights of 19th century Test cricket as well as one of its great characters. The first man to capture 50 wickets in Test matches, he also became the first to take a Test hat-trick when he dismissed the English batsmen Vernon Royle, Francis MacKinnon and Tom Emmett at Melbourne on 2 January 1879. The lofty and rather angular Spofforth had begun his bowling career delivering underarm lobs, as many did in those days, but changed to overarm when he saw what English bowlers could do. After much training he was able to bowl fast and fiercely, to the dismay of the batsmen of England. Having appeared in the second match of the first-ever Test series, he took 13 wickets in the third and in 1882 at The Oval finished with match figures of 14 for 90 as Australia won by seven runs despite totalling just 63 in their first innings. That inspirational performance is still the second best by an Australian in Tests, after Bob Massie's 16 for 137 in 1972, and it occurred in one of the closest-run Tests of all time. Spofforth eventually took ten wickets or more against England four times. His uncompromising approach to the game made him popular with followers but sometimes not so much with his opponents. He was, however, the model for countless cricketers who followed him, and the game owes him a great deal.

Born: Sydney, New South Wales, 9 September 1853
Died: Long Ditton, Surrey, 4 June 1926
Roles: Right-hand bat, right-arm fast-medium bowler
Teams: Victoria, New South Wales, Victoria, Australia
Ashes debut: 31 March 1877, Melbourne
Last Ashes appearance: 28 January 1887, Sydney
Ashes appearances: 18
Bowling: 94 wickets; average 18.41
Best bowling: 7/44
Batting: 217 runs; average 9.43
Highest score: 50
Fielding: 11 caught

Taylor

With a smile seldom far from his lips and a refreshingly positive approach to the game, Mark Taylor batted his way into Australian hearts and then captained his team to the top of the world. Under his captaincy, between 1994 and 1999, Australia played 50 Tests, won 26 of them and drew a further 11, leaving the next skipper, Steve Waugh, with the job of consolidating their position as world leaders. And all the while he was achieving team success, Taylor was also leading the way with the bat: opening the batting, he rattled up 19 Test centuries on his way to 7525 runs (average: 43.49), lending the Australian order an air of solidity that was reassuring and inspiring. His start in the Ashes could hardly have been more productive: his 136 and 60 on debut at Headingley went a long way towards giving Australia victory by 210 runs. Later in that series, at Nottingham, he led the way with 219 and did not have to bat again as England crumbled to an innings defeat. In all, the summer of 1989's six Tests saw him score a remarkable 839 runs at the equally remarkable average of 83.90. Taylor went on to score six hundreds in Ashes matches, supplementing them with 15 half-centuries. Another invaluable side to his game was his ultra-safe catching in the slips: his total of 157 Test match catches was a world record at the time. He retired to the commentary box safe in the knowledge that he had done a wonderful job.

Above: *Mark Taylor – successful with the bat and as a captain*

Born: Leeton, New South Wales, 27 October 1964
Roles: Left-hand bat, right-arm medium bowler
Teams: New South Wales, Victoria, Australia
Ashes debut: 8 June 1989, Leeds
Last Ashes appearance: 2 January 1999, Sydney
Ashes appearances: 33
Batting: 2496 runs; average 42.30
Highest score: 219
Fielding: 46 caught

Thomson

Right: *Jeff Thomson – slingshot action produced terrific pace and bounce*

It is doubtful whether anyone has ever bowled faster than Jeff Thomson at his most rapid. Speed guns and other gadgets recorded his deliveries at over 160 km/h (99.4 mph), but Thommo himself reckoned he could hit 180 km/h (111.9 mph). Whatever the truth, we know he could be very, very fast indeed. And he was awkward, too. His awe-inspiring slingshot action could produce tremendous bounce and deliveries that skidded on to a batsman who had no time to pick the direction of the ball, let alone react to it. With Dennis Lillee, Thomson formed one of the most formidable fast-bowling partnerships of all time; maybe even the best. The English tourists who played in the legendary Ashes of 1974/75 – before the days of helmets, let it be noted – were often simply terrorised into surrendering their wickets, and Thomson finished the series with 33 wickets at an average below 18. Memories of that winter haunted English batsmen for a long time, and Thomson was the gleeful taker of five English wickets in an innings five times in his career. Australian conditions suited him down to the ground but he took wickets wherever he went, ending up with 200 of them from his 51 Tests. His bowling style placed enormous strains on his body, and as time went on he was forced to reduce his pace and rely more on seam and swing than sheer speed. The wickets kept coming, though, and Thomson passed into cricket legend, where he will remain for ever.

Born: Sydney, New South Wales, 16 August 1950
Roles: Right-hand bat, right-arm fast bowler
Teams: New South Wales, Queensland, Middlesex, Australia
Ashes debut: 29 November 1974, Brisbane
Last Ashes appearance: 15 August 1985, Birmingham
Ashes appearances: 21
Bowling: 100 wickets; average 24.18
Best bowling: 6/46
Batting: 295 runs; average 14.75
Highest score: 49
Fielding: 9 caught

Trumble

Above: *Hugh Trumble – two hat-tricks in Tests*

Unbeaten as captain of Australia – he led the side twice – Hugh Trumble had another claim to fame: he was the first bowler to take two hat-tricks in Test matches. First, in 1902 at Melbourne, he disposed of the lower-order English batsmen Arthur Jones, John Gunn and Sydney Barnes in three balls, hastening Australian victory by 229 runs. Next, as an act of farewell in his final Test at Melbourne in 1904, he dismissed Bernard Bosanquet, Sir Pelham Warner and Dick Lilley with successive deliveries, again speeding his side to a big victory. Trumble was a tall off spinner with unusually long fingers who bowled at a brisk pace and had wonderful control over flight, speed and spin – and he was deadly on a wet wicket. He was also a very capable batsman who worked his way up the order until he was opening the innings, and passed the 50 mark on four occasions against England. But it was as a bowler that he was most often a match-winner. He captured 12 wickets in an Ashes match twice, managing the later of those feats at The Oval in 1902, when he contributed 71 undefeated runs and took 12 wickets for 173 – including eight for 65 in England's first innings – but finished on the losing side. We finish where we began, on Trumble's home ground of Melbourne, where he said goodbye to the Ashes with that hat-trick and a second-innings haul of seven for 28. Exit an outstanding cricketer.

Born: Melbourne, Victoria, 12 May 1867
Died: Melbourne, Victoria, 14 August 1938
Roles: Right-hand bat, right-arm off spin bowler
Teams: Victoria, Australia
Ashes debut: 21 July 1890, Lord's
Last Ashes appearance: 5 March 1904, Melbourne
Ashes appearances: 31
Bowling: 141 wickets; average 20.88
Best bowling: 8/65
Batting: 838 runs; average 19.95
Highest score: 70
Fielding: 45 caught

Trumper

Below: *Victor Trumper – idolised in his time*

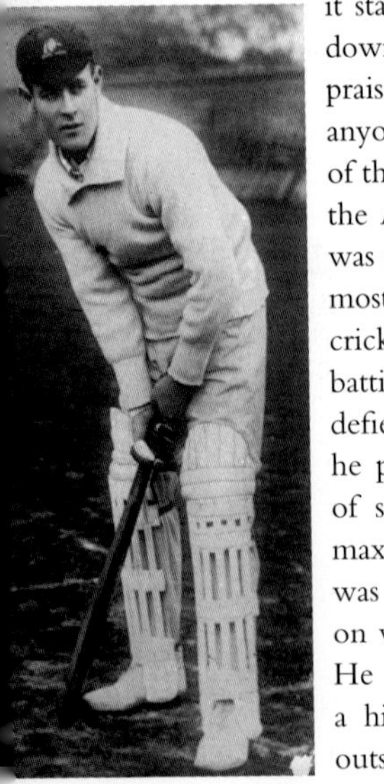

One of cricket's best-known photographs captures Victor Trumper in the act of stepping out to drive with a long, elegant stride, his bat lifted high and his eyes fixed on the ball. It takes little imagination to believe that ball ended up a very long way from where it started – as did a lot of deliveries sent down to one of the early game's most praised performers. It was no surprise to anyone when, in 1996, Trumper was one of the first ten players to be inducted into the Australian Cricket Hall of Fame. He was idolised in his time yet remained the most modest of players, and contemporary cricketers spoke in awed tones of his batting genius. CB Fry said Trumper defied all orthodox rules, 'yet every stroke he played satisfied the ultimate criterion of style – the minimum of effort, the maximum of effect.' Others noted that he was capable of making batting look easy on wickets that others found unplayable. He hit 3163 runs in his 48 Tests, with a highest score of 214 not out and an outstanding average for the time of 39.04. In Ashes matches he passed 100 six times, his highest score coming at Sydney in 1903 when he hit a faultless 185 not out in less than four hours. Even in his last Test, just three years before he died, he made a second-innings 50 as Australia chased an unlikely win. Victor Trumper went out as a hero.

Born: Sydney, New South Wales, 2 November 1877
Died: Sydney, New South Wales, 28 June 1915
Roles: Right-hand bat, right-arm medium bowler
Teams: New South Wales, Australia
Ashes debut: 1 June 1899, Nottingham
Last Ashes appearance: 23 February 1912, Sydney
Ashes appearances: 40
Batting: 2263 runs; average 32.79
Highest score: 185*
Bowling: 2 wickets; average 71.00
Best bowling: 2/35
Fielding: 25 caught

Turner

Although he had played against England – and destroyed more than one innings – before he left Australian shores for the Ashes tour of 1888, the English public really only woke up to the talents of Charlie Turner during that summer. The New South Welshman, a medium pacer with natural rhythm and a lethal off cutter, cut a swathe through the cricket teams of England on that tour, taking an almost unimaginable 283 wickets at the extraordinary average of 11.27. That total has only been bettered three times, each time by an Englishman, and will of course never be equalled again. Among Turner's wicket tally were the 17 he collected for 50 runs while playing an All-England XI at Hastings, and he finished the calendar year of 1888 with 314 dismissals. He had started his life in Test matches by whipping out six English batsmen for a mere 15 runs at Sydney in 1887, going on to dispatch 29 in the three matches of the series. His annus mirabilis of 1888 saw him accounting for 21 Englishmen in three Tests but, sadly, the miracles could not continue for ever. The Ashes series of 1892, 1893 and 1894 yielded wickets aplenty, but nothing on the scale of previous years. His last performances of note in Tests came in 1894 at Melbourne (match figures of eight for 131) and Sydney (seven for 51), and in his last match he became the first Australian to take 100 Test wickets. For that, a nation applauds.

Born: Bathurst, New South Wales, 16 November 1862
Died: Sydney, New South Wales, 1 January 1944
Roles: Right-hand bat, right-arm medium-fast bowler
Teams: New South Wales, Australia
Ashes debut: 28 January 1887, Sydney
Last Ashes appearance: 1 February 1895, Sydney
Ashes appearances: 17
Bowling: 101 wickets; average 16.53
Best bowling: 7/43
Batting: 323 runs; average 11.53
Highest score: 29
Fielding: 8 caught

Above: *Charlie Turner – 101 Ashes wickets in 17 matches*

Walters

Below: *Doug Walters – enormously valuable to Australian cricket*

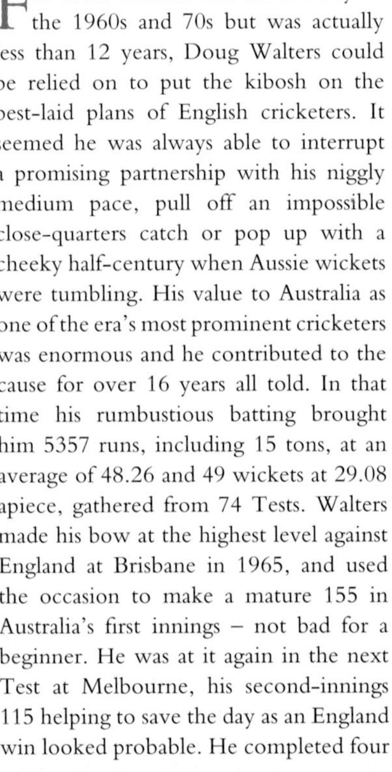

For what seemed like an eternity in the 1960s and 70s but was actually less than 12 years, Doug Walters could be relied on to put the kibosh on the best-laid plans of English cricketers. It seemed he was always able to interrupt a promising partnership with his niggly medium pace, pull off an impossible close-quarters catch or pop up with a cheeky half-century when Aussie wickets were tumbling. His value to Australia as one of the era's most prominent cricketers was enormous and he contributed to the cause for over 16 years all told. In that time his rumbustious batting brought him 5357 runs, including 15 tons, at an average of 48.26 and 49 wickets at 29.08 apiece, gathered from 74 Tests. Walters made his bow at the highest level against England at Brisbane in 1965, and used the occasion to make a mature 155 in Australia's first innings – not bad for a beginner. He was at it again in the next Test at Melbourne, his second-innings 115 helping to save the day as an England win looked probable. He completed four centuries and 13 fifties in Ashes matches, often after a lengthy night of carousing. He also pitched in twice with four wickets in an innings, his best figures coming at The Oval in 1975. Walters was the epitome of the hard-drinking, laid-back Aussie who played cricket as naturally and as easily as he lifted a schooner of beer. He was a hugely popular bloke and a phenomenal player.

Born: Dungog, New South Wales, 21 December 1945
Roles: Right-hand bat, right-arm medium bowler
Teams: New South Wales, Australia
Ashes debut: 10 December 1965, Brisbane
Last Ashes appearance: 25 August 1977, The Oval
Ashes appearances: 36
Batting: 1981 runs; average 35.37
Highest score: 155
Bowling: 26 wickets; average 28.07
Best bowling: 4/34
Fielding: 23 caught

Warne

No cricketer of the modern era has had such a profound influence on the game as Shane Warne. The mythology surrounding him is vast and he was feared, quite rightly, wherever he played. The first cricketer to take 700 Test wickets, he is often called the best bowler of all time, and who are we to argue? Warne was certainly the all-time master of leg spin, adding unerring accuracy to his weaponry of leg breaks, topspinners, flippers, googlies, sliders and goodness know what else. He added value with his seldom-heralded ability with the bat, with which he hit more than 3000 Test runs but never made it to a century, but it was his bowling the crowds flocked to see. No one can, or wants to, forget the delivery that introduced him to Ashes cricket, the ball that bowled a stunned Mike Gatting at Old Trafford in 1993. Warne's first ball against England pitched outside Gatting's leg stump before zipping past the watching batter to relieve his off stump of its bail. He went on to bewitch England for 13 long years, claiming 11 five-fors and recording his best match figures, 12 wickets for 246, in the magical Oval Test of 2005. It was with great satisfaction that he captured 23 wickets in the 2006/07 season as Australia snatched back the Ashes with a whitewash. There was nothing much left to prove after that, and Warne retired from Test cricket with 708 wickets, taken at 25.41 each, under his belt and his reputation for genius safe.

Above: *Shane Warne – often called the best bowler of all time*

Born: Ferntree Gully, Victoria, 13 September 1969
Roles: Right-hand bat, right-arm leg spin bowler
Teams: Victoria, Hampshire, Australia
Ashes debut: 3 June 1993, Manchester
Last Ashes appearance: 2 January 2007, Sydney
Ashes appearances: 36
Bowling: 195 wickets; average 23.25
Best bowling: 8/71
Batting: 946 runs; average 22.00
Highest score: 90
Fielding: 30 caught

Right:
Shane Warne acknowledges the applause after his final Test, against England at the Sydney Cricket Ground

Waugh, Mark

Above: *Mark Waugh (second left) – skills turned many a game*

Seldom has the Test arena been graced by a batting style so easy on the eye as Mark Waugh's. The younger of the Waugh twins, he hit a cricket ball as if it were the most natural thing in the world: a gorgeous cover drive here, a delightfully timed pull to the midwicket boundary there. The other departments of his game were similarly good-looking – his deceptively threatening bowling (he took 59 Test wickets) and his extraordinary athletic feats in the field turned many a game. 'Junior' entered Test cricket in 1991 in the grand style while mourning the dropping of twin brother Steve: his very first innings was a glorious 138 over which spectators and journalists drooled. It was the first century of six he was to hit in the Ashes. The last, a knock of 120 that Wisden called 'a thing of beauty', came in his final match against England in 2001 and was his 20th and last in Test cricket. Waugh hit 8029 runs in all Tests, putting him in fifth place in the all-time Australian run-scoring list, and the only slightly disappointing aspect of his record is that he never managed to get a really big score; his largest innings was the 153 not out he assembled in 1998 in India while suffering from fever and nausea. If you wanted to quibble you might also point to the occasions he seemed to lose focus and surrender his wicket too easily, but no one could dispute that Mark Waugh was a quite majestic cricketer.

Born: Sydney, New South Wales, 2 June 1965
Roles: Right-hand bat, right-arm medium and off spin bowler
Teams: New South Wales, Essex, Australia
Ashes debut: 25 January 1991, Adelaide
Last Ashes appearance: 23 August 2001, The Oval
Ashes appearances: 29
Batting: 2204 runs; average 50.09
Highest score: 140
Bowling: 14 wickets; average 37.07
Best bowling: 5/40
Fielding: 43 caught

Waugh, Steve

Below: *Steve Waugh – driven to succeed*

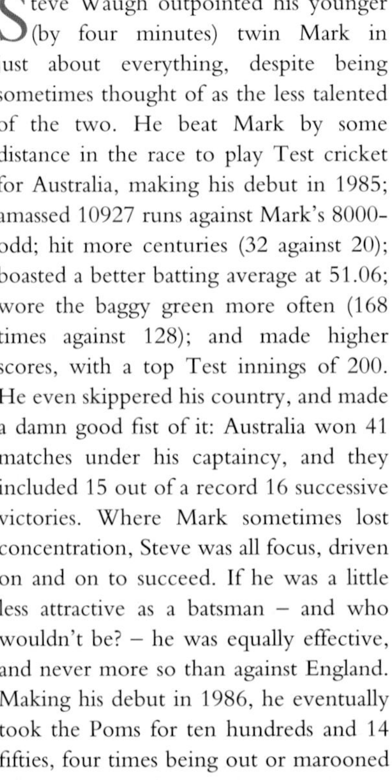

Steve Waugh outpointed his younger (by four minutes) twin Mark in just about everything, despite being sometimes thought of as the less talented of the two. He beat Mark by some distance in the race to play Test cricket for Australia, making his debut in 1985; amassed 10927 runs against Mark's 8000-odd; hit more centuries (32 against 20); boasted a better batting average at 51.06; wore the baggy green more often (168 times against 128); and made higher scores, with a top Test innings of 200. He even skippered his country, and made a damn good fist of it: Australia won 41 matches under his captaincy, and they included 15 out of a record 16 successive victories. Where Mark sometimes lost concentration, Steve was all focus, driven on and on to succeed. If he was a little less attractive as a batsman – and who wouldn't be? – he was equally effective, and never more so than against England. Making his debut in 1986, he eventually took the Poms for ten hundreds and 14 fifties, four times being out or marooned in the 90s. His highest score of 177 not out came quite early on, at Headingley in 1989, and was praised by Wisden as a reminder of a bygone age. Waugh's last big score in the Ashes was at The Oval in 2001 when, hampered by injury, he outscored his brother yet again – 157 not out to Mark's 120. Was this cricket's most fascinating sibling rivalry?

Born: Sydney, New South Wales, 2 June 1965
Roles: Right-hand bat, right-arm medium bowler
Teams: New South Wales, Somerset, Ireland, Kent, Australia
Ashes debut: 14 November 1986, Brisbane
Last Ashes appearance: 2 January 2003, Sydney
Ashes appearances: 46
Batting: 3200 runs; average 58.18
Highest score: 177*
Bowling: 22 wickets; average 41.54
Best bowling: 5/69
Fielding: 29 caught

Woodfull

Above: *Bill Woodfull (left) with Vic Richardson – a steady accumulator of runs*

Bill Woodfull will forever be associated with the Bodyline tour of 1932/33, when the English fast bowlers were instructed to bowl short on the line of the batsman's leg stump, with devastating results for batters' bodies and diplomatic relations. The Australian captain and opening bat, despite on one occasion being laid low by a blow to the heart, refused to complain or retaliate, and his dignified behaviour won him many admirers. There was an awful lot more to Woodfull than that nasty Bodyline business, however. Calmness personified, he was a steady accumulator of runs whose defence was famously hard to penetrate and who scored 2300 runs in Test cricket, with seven centuries, 13 fifties and an average of 46.00. Australian teams under his captaincy won 14 and drew four of 25 Tests, and regained the Ashes twice. Six of Woodfull's Test hundreds were compiled against England, whose bowling often foundered on the rock of his partnership with Bill Ponsford. Patience was his forte, and he displayed it in spades when he scored 155 at Lord's in 1930 as he and Ponsford wore down the English bowlers in preparation for Don Bradman to come in and smite 254. Yet he will always be remembered for his restrained reply to England's manager, Plum Warner, who had come to Australia's dressing room to commiserate after Woodfull's felling by Harold Larwood at Adelaide in 1933: 'I do not want to see you, Mr Warner. There are two teams out there. One is playing cricket and the other is not.'

Born: Maldon, Victoria, 22 August 1897
Died: Tweed Heads South, New South Wales, 11 August 1965
Roles: Right-hand bat
Teams: Victoria, Australia
Ashes debut: 12 June 1926, Nottingham
Last Ashes appearance: 18 August 1934, The Oval
Ashes appearances: 25
Batting: 1675 runs; average 44.07
Highest score: 155
Fielding: 5 caught

ALSO IN THIS SERIES

GRAND PRIX
DRIVER BY DRIVER

A COMPILATION OF THE TOP 100 GRAND PRIX DRIVERS

LIAM McCANN

ALSO IN THIS SERIES

SNOOKER
PLAYER BY PLAYER

A COMPILATION OF THE 100 GREATEST SNOOKER PLAYERS

LIAM McCANN

ALSO IN THIS SERIES

ENGLAND
PLAYER BY PLAYER

A COMPILATION OF THE 100 GREATEST ENGLAND PLAYERS

GRAHAM BETTS

ALSO IN THIS SERIES

BRITISH AND IRISH LIONS PLAYER BY PLAYER

A COMPILATION OF THE 100 GREATEST BRITISH AND IRISH LIONS PLAYERS

LIAM McCANN

FOREWORD BY TOM SMITH

The pictures in this book were provided courtesy of the following:

GETTY IMAGES
101 Bayham Street, London NW1 0AG

WIKICOMMONS
commons.wikimedia.org

Design & Artwork by: Scott Giarnese & Alex Young

Published by: Demand Media Limited & G2 Entertainment Limited

Publishers: Jason Fenwick & Jules Gammond

The Story of the Urn written by: Ralph Dellor and Stephen Lamb

Written by: Pat Morgan